د افغانستان پښتو متلونه

Mataluna:
151 Afghan Pashto Proverbs

Collected and translated by
Captain Edward Zellem
United States Navy

Edited by
Hares Ahmadzai

Illustrated by
The students of Marefat High School
Kabul, Afghanistan

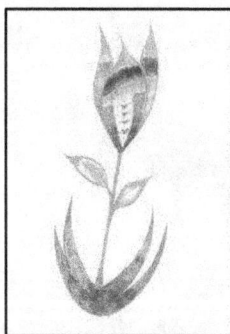

Dedication
خانګړی شوی

This book is respectfully dedicated
to the people of Afghanistan,
and to those who have given their lives
to bring lasting peace and security.
May Almighty God bless and protect them,
and bring them success.

دا کتاب د افغانستان عزتمند ولس ته او هغه کسانو ته چی
خپل ژوندونه یی د تل پاتی سولی راوستلو او د امنیت
تینګښت لپاره له لاسه ورکړی، خانګړی شوی ده. د الله
(ج) له درباره هغوی ته مغفرت همدارنګه نور د په خپل
پناه کښی وساتی او هغوی ته بریالیتوب ورپه برخه کړی.

As the Proverb says:

لکه دغه متل چی وایی:

که غر لوردی په سر لارلري.

Kha ghar lwar day pe sar laar lray.

Even if a mountain is very high, there is a path to the top.

ستړی مشی
Staray mashay
Be Tireless

Table of Contents

لیک لر

Preface

سریزه

THE AFGHAN PROVERBS SERIES

Many people around the world were surprised when my first book, *Zarbul Masalha: 151 Afghan Dari Proverbs*, became popular so soon after it was published internationally in 2012.

I was not one of the surprised. I knew that a bilingual book of Afghan *zarbul masalha* ('Proverbs' in Dari) had much to offer. But I *was* surprised to learn that so little had been written in the West about Afghan Proverbs. As a Dari speaker who had collected and used Afghan Proverbs daily in Afghanistan for a year and a half, I knew how important proverbs are in Afghan culture and speech. I also knew how important Afghan Proverbs are for understanding Afghans and building relationships with them. I was certain that non-Afghans would like the proverbs too.

But even I didn't yet fully understand how true this was.

After *Zarbul Masalha* was published, people all over the world began contacting me with their stories. 40,000 copies of *Zarbul Masalha*'s first edition (Kabul: Karwan Press, 2011) were being used by Afghan students studying Dari and English in over 200 schools across Afghanistan. Nancy Dupree's world-renowned Afghanistan Centre at Kabul University (ACKU) distributed hundreds of copies to villages throughout Afghanistan through its nationwide ABLE 'books-in-a box' mobile library program. Social workers in Europe began using *Zarbul Masalha* to help integrate Afghan refugees and immigrants into their new societies. A young Afghan woman had an idea to build a small reading room in Kabul, and used dozens of copies to attract readers and promote literacy for Afghan youth.

People around the world also were excited by the 50 original paintings and drawings by the Afghan high school students who illustrated *Zarbul Masalha*. These artworks were created in collaboration with Marefat High School in Kabul, and were the students' own original conceptions of Afghan Proverbs through art.

The student artists of *Zarbul Masalha: 151 Afghan Dari Proverbs*

GLOBAL ATTENTION ON AFGHAN PROVERBS

Members of the Afghan Diaspora - especially émigré parents of young children born overseas - were especially entranced by the combination of art, words and meaning in *Zarbul Masalha*. Many of them asked for a large-print, full-color edition to help their children learn Dari and other languages. This soon became *Afghan Proverbs Illustrated*, and then a series published in additional languages.

After the English-Dari edition of *Afghan Proverbs Illustrated* was published in 2012, volunteers from around the world offered to translate it into their own native languages. This became a series of Afghan Proverbs books in over a dozen third languages that included German, Dutch, French, Swedish, Greek, Spanish, Italian, Portuguese, Russian, Finnish, Polish, and Romanian. The *Afghan Proverbs Illustrated* book series continues to grow, and like *Zarbul Masalha* is now available in over 70 countries through Amazon.com, The Book Depository, and many other leading international booksellers. More information and details can be found at www.afghansayings.com.

Zarbul Masalha and *Afghan Proverbs Illustrated* also began winning national and international book awards. *Zarbul Masalha* won a Gold Medal from the Military Writers Society of America (2013, Reference category). *Afghan Proverbs Illustrated* won First Place in the 21st Annual Writer's Digest Self-Published Book Awards (2013, Reference) and an IPPY Bronze Medal from the 18th Annual Independent Publisher Book Awards (2014, Multicultural Non-Fiction – Juvenile/Young Adult). At the time of this writing, both books were finalists in competition for several other book awards.

Professors and researchers in the field of *paremiology* also began to take note. Paremiology is the scientific study of proverbs, and is a specialized field of ethnolinguistics studied in universities and other centers of learning all over the world. In 2013, I was honored with election to the prestigious *Associação Internacional de Paremiologia* (International Association of Paremiology/AIP-IAP). The AIP-IAP is based in Tavira, Portugal, a city that is known internationally as 'The World Capital of Proverbs.'

I spoke later that year in Tavira to the AIP-IAP's 7th Annual Interdisciplinary Colloquium on Proverbs (ICP-13). Delegates representing 22 nations were very interested, because to date so little formal paremiological or *paremiographical* (collection of proverbs) work has been done on Afghan Proverbs. With the publication of *Zarbul Masalha*, the *Afghan Proverbs Illustrated* series, and now this book, that is beginning to change.

A QUESTION AND A CHALLENGE

As the Afghan Proverbs books continued to gain global attention, one of the most common questions I encountered was from Afghans who speak Pashto. Afghanistan has two official languages, Dari and Pashto, and about half of all Afghans speak Pashto as their first language. There also are millions of Pashto speakers in

Pakistan, just across Afghanistan's southern border. The question these proud Pashtuns often asked me was: *When will you write a Pashto Proverbs book?*

I knew this was a very important question. Such a book had to be written as a companion edition for *Zarbul Masalha*. Pashto *Mataluna* ('Proverbs' in Pashto) are just as vital and commonly used in the Pashto language as *zarbul masalha* are for Dari speakers.

The issue for me was how to write a book of Pashto Proverbs, and the challenge had two parts to overcome. First, I was not a Pashto speaker. As a trained Dari speaker living in Afghanistan, it had been easy and natural for me to collect, translate and use Dari *zarbul masalha* during my daily conversations with Afghans in their own language. I couldn't do it that way again with Pashto *mataluna*. Although Pashto and Dari share some similarities, they are two very different languages.

The second challenge was how physically to collect the *mataluna*, since I was no longer in Afghanistan and was living half a world away.

Not surprisingly, I found the answer in a very popular and famous Afghan Proverb that is shared in both Dari and Pashto:

په یو ګل نه پسرلی کیږي.

Pa yau gul na pesarlay kigi.
(Pashto, *Mataluna* p. 64)

به یک گل، بهار نمی‌شه.

Ba yak gul, bahaar nameysha.
(Dari, *Zarbul Masalha* p. 115)

This Pashto *matal* and its matching Dari *zarbul masal* both have the same meaning. They translate as '*One flower doesn't bring spring*' and are Afghan Proverbs of cooperation and teamwork. They mean that it is very hard for one person to accomplish a big project alone.

With these two proverbs in mind, I developed a 21st century solution to the challenges of language and geography. The answer was *crowdsourcing for content* using social media, the World Wide Web, and mobile phones. Although many Afghans still lack regular access to desktop computers and broadband Internet, I knew from personal observation that almost every Afghan has access to mobile phones. And that access to mobile phones would give me access to Afghans through Twitter and other social media.

When I proposed my idea of 'crowdsourcing proverbs' to experts from the AIP-IAP, many said that this method appears to be unprecedented in paremiology and paremiography. They also saw my crowdsourcing idea as a new way to explore the *paremiological minimum* for the Pashto language. The idea of a 'paremiological minimum' is attributed to the Russian paremiologist Grigorii Permyakov, who in 1979 defined it as *the core baseline of proverbs that almost all members of a society can be expected to know*. For example, most adult Americans are familiar with the proverb 'the squeaky wheel gets the grease,' so that proverb is considered part of the American paremiological minimum.

However, my main goal remained to collect, translate, illustrate and publish 151 Pashto Proverbs that are commonly used in today's Afghanistan. If that helped add to the academic body of knowledge on the Afghan paremiological minimum, so much the better.

CROWDSOURCING AFGHAN PROVERBS

Crowdsourcing is a method that became popular online in the early 21st century. According to Merriam-Webster, the first known use of the word was in 2006 to combine the concepts of *crowds* and *outsourcing*.

In practice, crowdsourcing today is most often seen as a way for individuals or groups to raise money by asking for small donations from a large group of people via the Internet. Online services such as Kickstarter, Crowdrise, GoFundMe and Indiegogo have been developed to support these crowdsourcers, whose goal is often to fund small personal projects for charity. However, crowdsourcing (also called *crowdfunding*) also has been used to raise money for projects by independent filmmakers, musicians and even small business startups.

But what I needed most to write a bilingual book of Pashto Proverbs wasn't money, it was *content* – the proverbs themselves. The *mataluna* had to be in common use by Afghan Pashtuns today, and I needed 151 of them in Pashto with literal English translations and transliterations.

Thanks to my first two books of Afghan Dari Proverbs and an ever-growing global network of followers on my website (afghansayings.com), Twitter (@afghansayings), and Facebook, I already had a very active online base. So I created a *mataluna* collection page called 'The Pashto Proverbs Project' on my website and began to crowdsource. Friends and fans of Afghan Proverbs started spreading the word online, and soon many fresh, popular, and meaningful contributions of Pashto Proverbs started flowing in. They came from native Pashto speakers in Afghanistan, Pakistan and over a dozen other nations.

Soon I had far more *mataluna* than the 151 that I needed. Some were in several different Pashto dialects, and I wanted to ensure that all of them were understood and commonly used in today's Afghanistan. So I began operationally testing the crowdsourced *mataluna* with daily tweets using the Twitter handle @afghansayings and hashtag #AfghanProverbs. The number of followers on Twitter grew fast, and they were not shy about commenting on and retweeting my Pashto Proverbs tweets. I was able to assess quickly from the number of retweets, favorites and comments if a particular *matal* was popular and correctly translated.

EDITING AND ILLUSTRATION

I also needed an expert editor to verify my collection. I found one in Hares Ahmadzai (p.155), a native speaker of Afghan Pashto and fluent in several other languages. He generously volunteered his services to the project, and soon we had selected and validated 151 of the best crowdsourced Afghan Pashto Proverbs.

Then I sent my list to Marefat High School (MHS) in Kabul, home of the talented student illustrators of *Zarbul Masalha: 151 Afghan Dari Proverbs.* After our earlier successes with the Dari Proverbs books, Marefat was as excited as I was about creating and illustrating a companion book of Pashto Proverbs. Repeating the model we used for *Zarbul Masalha*, the MHS faculty and students selected 50 of their favorite *mataluna* from my list. Painting them became part of the MHS Art Department's curriculum in the fall of 2013. In addition to being a fun and useful learning experience for the students, the school's "Charity Box" was compensated for this work with royalties from the earlier Dari Proverbs books. As an important side benefit, this helped with tuition assistance for some of Marefat's neediest students. (More about Marefat High School on page 153).

The result of this unprecedented international team – the native Pashto speakers from around the world who contributed crowdsourced *mataluna*, and the student illustrators and faculty of Marefat High School in our second major collaboration – has now become this book.

ACKNOWLEDGEMENTS AND MANANA مننه (THANKS)

په یو ګل نه پسرلی کیږي.

Pa yau gul na pesarlay kigi.
One flower doesn't bring spring.

There are so many 'flowers' who brought spring to this project that it is impossible to list them all by name, but they all know who they are. I am greatly in their debt, and I have been privileged to know them and work with them. Their generosity of spirit and action in support of Afghan literacy, languages and human understanding across cultures has been moving and humbling.

I would particularly like thank the following individuals and organizations for their contributions, support and inspiration:

- The hundreds of native Pashto speakers around the world who contributed their favorite *mataluna* to the Pashto Proverbs crowdsourcing project on behalf of all Pashtuns and all Afghans.
- The faculty, parents and student artists of **Marefat High School** in Kabul, who helped bring to life *Zarbul Masalha, Afghan Proverbs Illustrated*, and now this book with their beautiful and insightful illustrations.
- My good friend **Aziz Royesh**, a founder and faculty member of Marefat High School and an emerging national voice for peace, education and development in Afghanistan.
- **Hares Ahmadzai**, the editor of this book. Mr. Ahmadzai is a native Pashto speaker and is fluent in several languages. He spent many hours reviewing my manuscript of crowdsourced *mataluna* to ensure that the spelling, translation, and transliteration were correct and that each *matal* is commonly used in Afghanistan today. Also, Mr. Ahmadzai's respected father **Major General Ghulam Sakhi Ahmadzai** will always be one of my dearest Afghan friends.
- The late **Qazi Ahmad Jan M.B.E.** (1883-1951) and his grandson **Ali Jan**, who contributed a number of *mataluna* to this project from the unpublished notebooks of the great "*Munshi* of Peshawar." Ph.D candidate **Noor ul Basar ('Aman')** helped Ali Jan select and translate *mataluna* from the Qazi's treasured notebooks, all of which were more than 70 years old. (p. 156)

- **General David H. Petraeus** (USA, ret.), **General John R. Allen** (USMC, ret.), **General James N. Mattis** (USMC, ret.), and **Nancy Dupree** of the Afghanistan Centre at Kabul University (ACKU), whose early interest and encouragement for my personal project with Afghan Proverbs remains a daily inspiration.
- Dozens of journalists such as **Howard Altman** (Tampa Tribune), **Cathryn J. Prince** (Christian Science Monitor), **Lina Rozbih** and **Jila Samee** (Voice of America), **Ariadne Bechthold** (Afghan Voice FM, London), **Mari Yusef** (Radio Azad), **Hadi Nili** (BBC Persian), **Amanullah Atta** (BBC Pashto), **Frank Wuco** (Fox NewsRadio), **Sahar Jaan** (Payam-e Afghan TV), **Mari Yusef** (Radio Azad), **Beth Underwood** (The Blaze), **Chauncey Ross** and **Carl Kologie** (Indiana Gazette), **Dr. Farid Younos** (NOOOR-TV), **Dwight Jon Zimmerman** (Veterans Radio Network), and other media personalities who have helped bring the Afghan Proverbs series to a global audience.
- Members of the **Associação Internacional de Paremiologia (International Association of Paremiology (AIP-IAP)** and AIP-IAP president **Dr Rui Soares**, who introduced me to the formal sciences of paremiology and paremiography and continue to provide me with education and advice. (p. 161)
- The volunteer translators of *Afghan Proverbs Illustrated* from the original English-Dari into bilingual editions in their own native languages. All these books are world-firsts, and the translators have made significant contributions to Afghan languages, their own languages, and to better understanding between cultures and nations.
- The great Afghan art historian and artist **Hamid Naweed**, author of *Art Through the Ages in Afghanistan* and a trusted mentor and friend. Two of his original works depicting the poet Rahman Baba and Afghan heroine Malalai of Maiwand

are featured in this book. **Amin Muftoon** contributed his sketch *The Flower*, which is drawn in the Kandahari style and is featured on many pages of *Mataluna*.

- My late mother and father, who grew to love Afghan Proverbs as much as any Afghan, and my late brother **Lt. Cmdr. Scott Zellem, U.S. Navy** (1968-2004) who would have loved Afghan Proverbs too. *Mahroona marhee kho nomona eh pah-ta-kee-jhee.* ميرونه مري خو نومونه يي پاتي كيږي. 'The brave die, but their legends remain forever.' R.I.P.

- **Dr. Peter Unseth** of the Graduate Institute of Applied Linguistics and **Dr. Wolfgang Mieder** of the University of Vermont, whose mentorship, encouragement and scientific work in paremiology have been an education and inspiration.

- Afghan food and culture writer **Humaira Ghilzai**, who graciously agreed to write the Foreword to *Mataluna* (p.xii).

- One of many perspectives that Afghans and Americans share is a deep and abiding love of family. Special thanks to my **wife**, **children** and **sister**, without whose love, patience and support my books would never have been written.

Finally, I would like to dedicate this book to my many good and respected Afghan friends, who helped me to discover Afghan Proverbs through our daily social interactions and work together both in Afghanistan and in cyberspace. I am deeply grateful for their friendship, help and wisdom, and especially for their efforts to build a secure and free Afghanistan.

With best regards,
Edward Zellem
ادوارد زالم

Rahman Baba - Pashtun Poet (1653-1711)
By Hamid Naweed

Foreword
سرلیک

'A nation stays alive when its culture stays alive.'
- Inscription at the National Museum of Afghanistan, Kabul

My friend Edward Zellem has re-engaged Afghans with the ancient art of their rich languages through his bilingual books *Zarbul Masalha: 151 Afghan Dari Proverbs, Afghan Proverbs Illustrated,* and now *Mataluna: 151 Afghan Pashto Proverbs.*

I grew up in Afghanistan with my father spouting proverbs at any teachable moment. However, when the Russians invaded in 1979 my family fled Afghanistan. In our efforts to survive as new immigrants to the United States, my parents took on odd jobs and worked endless hours - leaving very little time for preserving our connection with Afghanistan or my father's proverbs. I embraced my American life by trading in Dari for English, reading Judy Blume, and swapping my Ahmad Zahir tapes for Duran Duran.

پشت هر تاریکی، روشنی است.
Pusht e har taareekee, roshanee ast.
After every darkness, there is light.

In the past 35 years, Afghanistan has held the title of the largest refugee-producing country in the world, with almost six million emigrating to neighboring countries Pakistan and Iran, and another two million scattering to many other countries around the world. This period in Afghan history has stunted the nation's natural cultural evolution and growth. In addition to the Afghans in Afghanistan who have lived through decades of war and instability, there are now three generations born overseas to Afghan parents in the Afghan Diaspora. Many of them have little tangible connection to their past, their language or their heritage.

غر په غر نه ورځي، خو بنده په بنده ورځي.
Ghar pa ghar na warzi, kho banda pa banda warzi.
Mountains do not draw nearer to each other, but people do.

While traveling in Afghanistan I found that most young Afghans knew much more about their differences than their commonalities. Aside from the well-known narratives of bombs, guns, and death, the less-tangible effect of war is the breakdown of a nation's core identity, which plays a detrimental role in postwar recovery.

علم تاج سر است.

Elm taaj-e sar ast.

Knowledge is a crown on the head.

Since 2001, there have been extensive efforts to rebuild the Afghan educational system, preserve cultural heritage sites, and re-engage Afghans in the future of their country. Today millions of Afghan children are attending school, but Afghanistan still has the lowest literacy rate in the world. The staggering reality of illiteracy in Dari and Pashto also plagues many Afghans in the Diaspora, especially those born outside Afghanistan.

له زړه نه بل زړه ته لار شته.

La zra na bal zra ta laar shta.

From one heart to another, there is a way.

Sometimes, knowledge comes from the most unexpected sources. Edward Zellem's books of Dari and Pashto Proverbs have created common ground for Afghans who are worlds apart to reconnect through their natural love of Proverbs.

Now, I can be sitting in my home in San Francisco, highlighting and reading *Mataluna*, while a woman in Ghazni could be cradling her baby while looking at the same exact page – both of us struggling with parsing the letters of وطن په خلکو ښايسته وي 'Watan pah khalkoo shayestah we.'

One's nation is only made beautiful by the people in it.

Humaira Ghilzai *

* **Humaira Ghilzai** is well-known in the Afghan Diaspora as one of the world's top Afghan food and culture writers. Her focus is on bridging the gaps of mutual understanding between the West and the people of Afghanistan. As part of her many efforts to improve the lives of Afghans, Ms. Ghilzai co-founded the Afghan Friends Network (AFN) in 2003 and the Hayward-Ghazni 'Sister City' initiative in 2005, where she has spearheaded critical programs to improve education for Afghan women, girls and boys, particularly in Afghanistan's Ghazni province.

Ms. Ghilzai writes about Afghan culture and cuisine on her widely popular website *Afghan Culture Unveiled* (www.afghancooking.net). She also gives frequent lectures about Afghanistan, and has served as cultural consultant for stage productions of *The Kite Runner*, *Blood and Gifts*, *Love in Afghanistan*, and a Hollywood movie.

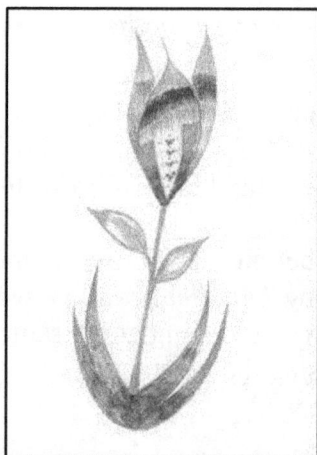

Malalai in the Battle of Maiwand
By Hamid Naweed

Pashto Language Facts

د پښتو ژبی په هکله څو ټکی

- Pashto is one of the two official languages of Afghanistan; the other is Dari. About 40 million people speak Pashto as a first language.

- The majority of Pashto native speakers live in Afghanistan (12 million) and northwest Pakistan (27 million). Statistics vary widely. Pashto speakers also are found in India, Iran, Tajikistan, and many other countries.

- Pashto has many dialects. Most language scholars classify them in 4 major groups: a Western dialect (Kandahari Pashto); an Eastern dialect (Nangarhari or Peshawari Pashto); a Central Dialect (spoken in Kabul, Parwan, Logar, Ghazni); and a Southern dialect (Paktika and Paktia).

- Pashto is considered part of the Indo-European family of languages. It is very different from the Persian languages (Dari, Farsi and Tajik). Most Afghans are bilingual to a degree in Pashto and Dari. However, it is much more common for a native Pashto speaker to speak excellent Dari than it is for a native Dari speaker to speak excellent Pashto.

- Today's Pashto has been influenced by many Persian and non-Persian languages from across Central and South Asia, making it particularly interesting for ethnolinguists to study.

- Pashto as spoken in Afghanistan has been influenced by Dari and shares some of its vocabulary. Some loaned words also have come to Pashto from Arabic, and some Indian words have come to it through Urdu.

- Pashto script is based on Arabic script with additional letters for sounds unique to Pashto. Like Dari and Arabic, Pashto is written and read from right to left. Also like Dari and Arabic, there are no distinct capital or lower case letters.

- There are 44 letters in the Pashto alphabet with a total of 37 sounds.

- Like many other languages, Pashto has both formal and informal (familiar) usage that includes different vocabulary. Also like some other languages, Pashto uses feminine and masculine genders.

- Pashto is written in a cursive or script style. The shape of a letter can change depending on whether it is found at the beginning, middle or end of a word. A letter also can change shape depending on what letter combinations precede or follow it.

Pronunciation Guide
رهنمای تلفظ

Each Proverb in *Mataluna* is numbered, and is presented in at least four lines. This is useful for both language students and general readers. The following format is used to present each entry:

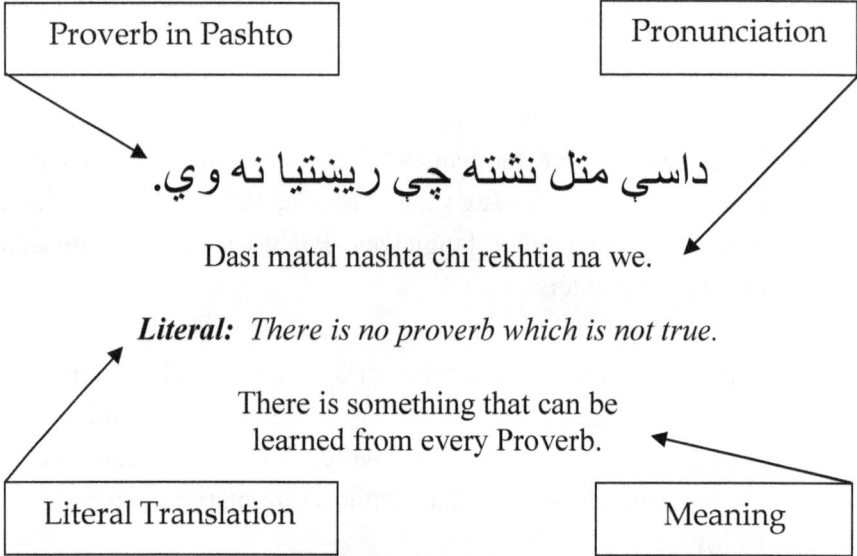

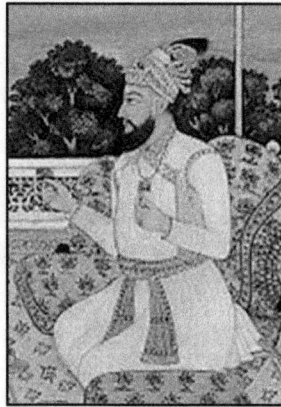

Proverb in Pashto	Pronunciation

داسي متل نشته چي ريښتيا نه وي.

Dasi matal nashta chi rekhtia na we.

Literal: *There is no proverb which is not true.*

There is something that can be
learned from every Proverb.

Literal Translation	Meaning

Phonetic Pronunciation Key
د تلفظ لارنبونه

- "kh" is a "k" sound combined with "h" sound, made in the back of the throat as if clearing it.
- "oy" rhymes with "boy."
- "e" when attached to the end of a word sounds like "ay," as in "hay."
- "r" is a roll of the "r" sound across the tongue.
- "ey/ay" rhymes with "hay."
- "mey" sounds like "may" with a soft "y" sound.
- "gh" is a "g" sound combined with an "h" sound, made in the back of the throat as if clearing it.
- "aa" sounds like "Au," as in "August."
- "q" is a "q" sound combined with a soft "h" sound, made in the back of the throat as if clearing it.

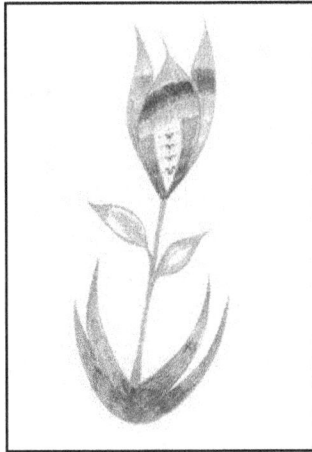

The Pashto Alphabet

د پښتو الفبا توری

ج	ث	ټ	ت	پ	ب	ا
jeem	say	tee	tey	pey	bey	alef
(j/dj)	(s)	(tt)	(t)	(p)	(b)	(aa/a)
ډ	د	خ	ح	څ	ځ	چ
daal	daal	xey	hey	cey	dzey	chey
(dd)	(d)	(x, ch)	(h)	(c)	(dz/j/z)	(ch)
س	ږ	ژ	ز	ړ	ر	ذ
seen	gey	zhey	zey	rey	rey	zaal
(s)	(gee/zee)	(zh)	(z)	(rr)	(r)	(z)
ع	ظ	ط	ض	ص	ڼ	ش
ayn	zoy	toy	dwad/zwad	suwat	xheen	sheen
(e)	(z)	(t)	(d/z)	(s)	(xh/sh)	(sh)
م	ل	ګ	ک	ق	ف	غ
meem	laam	gaaf	kaaf	qaf	fey	ghayn
(m)	(l)	(g)	(k)	(q)	(f)	(gh)
ي	ي	ى	ه	و	ڼ	ن
majhula	marufa	mulayyana hey		wow	nuun	noon
ye (ay/y)	ye (ee)	ye (y/ay)	(h,ah)	(w/u/o)	(nn)	(n)
		ئ		ى		
		karwala ye		xeena ye		
		(ay/y)		(ay/ei)		

خپله لاسه ګله لاسه.

Khpala laasa gula laasa.

Literal: The labor of one's own hand is beautiful.

The fruits of your own work are sweeter because you have earned them. It is better to do things for yourself rather than to rely on other people for help.

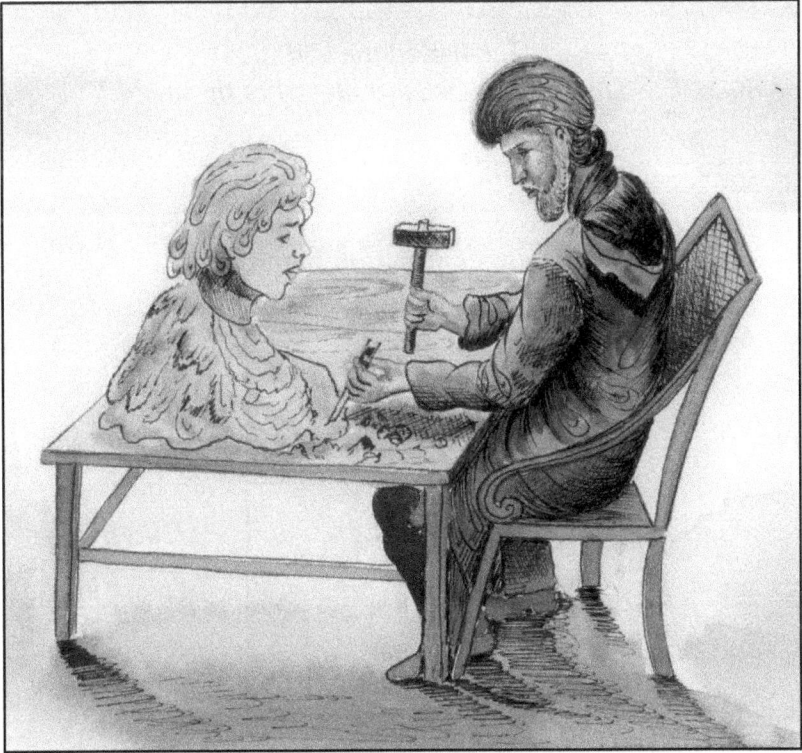

مور په یو لاس زانګو، او
په بل لاس نړۍ زنګوي.

Mor pa yau laas zango, au pa bal laas naray zangawi.

Literal: *A mother rocks the cradle with one hand,*
and the world with the other hand.

Mothers are very important and always must be respected. By raising their children, mothers shape the future of the world.

English equivalent:
"The hand that rocks the cradle rules the world."

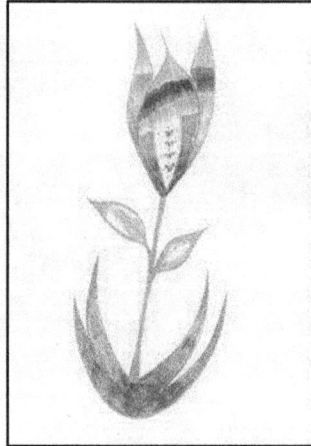

ښنګه چي غريږي، هسې نه وريږي.

Sanga che ghorigi, hase na worigi.

Literal: *It does not rain the way it thunders.*

Things are not usually as bad or frightening as they may seem
at first glance. Be brave, and always have hope for the best.

English equivalent: "A dog's bark is worse than its bite."

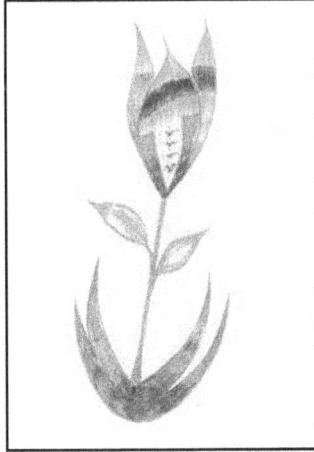

بنده ته حرکت کوه زه به برکت کؤوم.

Banda ta harkat kawa za ba barakat kawoom.

Literal: *If people act, God will bless them.*

Glamorous conversation or mere wishes are not enough to make things happen. A person also must take action. God blesses people who work hard to attain their goals.

English equivalent: "God helps those who help themselves."

ارزان بي علته نه وي،
ګران بي حکمته نه وي.

Arzaan be elata na wi, graan be hekmata na wi.

Literal: There is a reason why one thing
is cheap, and another is expensive.

Things that are worth more usually cost more time, effort or
money. Everything has its own unique quality and value.

English equivalent: "You get what you pay for."

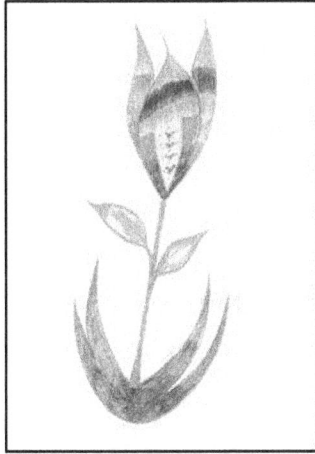

هر څه چی ډیر شي نو ګنډیر شي.

Har sa che der shi no gander shi.

Literal: *Too much of anything is poisonous.*

Moderation is important, even with good things. Even healthy things can be harmful in large quantities. Excess in anything can be bad for the body, mind or spirit.

English equivalent: "Moderation in all things."
(often attributed to the Greek philosopher Aristotle.)

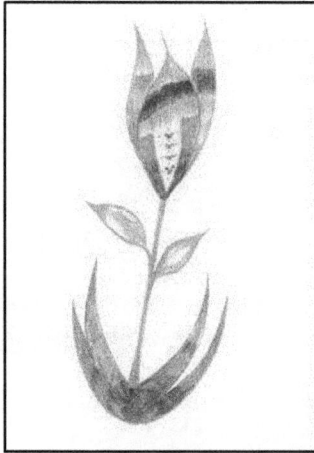

غوا که توره ده شیدی یي سپینی دي.

Ghwaa ka tora da shedy yee speenye dee.

Literal: *Although a cow is black, her milk is white.*

Do not judge things or people by outward appearances alone.
Look deeper first, and without prejudice.
What is inside is what counts.

English equivalents: "You can't judge a book by its cover"
and "Beauty is only skin deep."

دوست به دي وژروي،
دبنمن به دي وخندوي.

Dost ba dee wozharawi, dukhman ba dee wokhandawi.

Literal: *A friend makes you cry, an enemy makes you laugh.*

Friends tell the truth, even if it may not be what you want to
hear or makes you feel uncomfortable. Enemies will trick you
and make you think everything is fine, even if it is not.

Also: Harsh words from a friend can hurt a person
much more than the same words from an enemy.

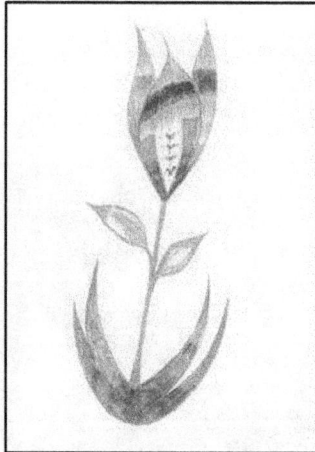

د صبر میوه خوږه ده.

Da sabr mewa khwaga da.

Literal: *Fruits you have waited for are sweet.*

Be patient, especially in difficult times, and good things may happen. Always be hopeful and never despair. Good things need time to grow, so let them evolve naturally.

English equivalent:
"Good things come to those who wait."

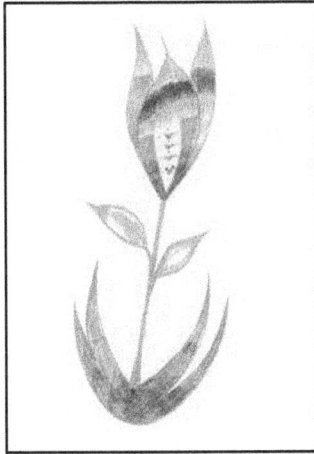

واده آسان وي خو تک توک ئي گران وي.

Waada asaan we kho tak tuk yi graan we.

Literal: *A wedding ceremony is easy, but the preparation is hard.*

It is important to lay the proper groundwork for
what you want to do. If you plan, work hard
and prepare, things usually will go well.

(*Note:* This proverb also is used when people wish for
something, but forget that work is required to get it.)

د وچو سره لامده هم سوځي.

Da wacho sara lamdah hm swazee.

Literal: Wet also burns with the dry.

Everyone suffers when there is a big problem
or disaster, both good people and bad people.

Also: If you keep bad company, when they get in trouble you
will probably get in trouble too – even if you are innocent.

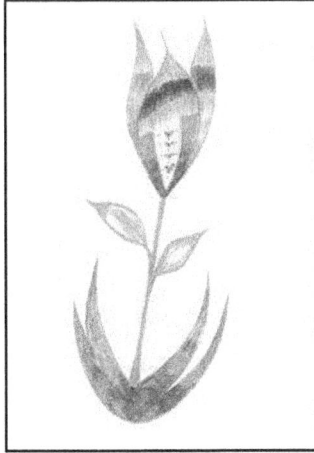

اوبه په ډانګ نه بېلېږي.

Uba pa daang na beligi.

Literal: *Water cannot be divided with a club.*

What belongs together will join naturally and stay together.
Brute force cannot keep apart what is destined
or meant by nature to be together.

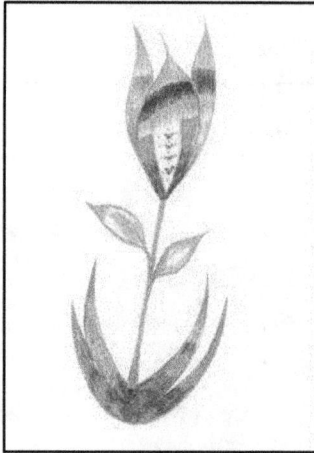

ژرنده که د پلار، ده هم په وار ده.

Zhranda ka de plaar da ham pa waar da.

Literal: *Even if the flour mill is your father's,*
you still have to wait your turn.

Do not take shortcuts at others' expense just because you are
powerful or have status. Do not cut in line or take shortcuts
just because you or your family are influential. Be fair.

د بوسو لاندې اوبه مه تیروه.

Da boso laanday oba ma terawa.

Literal: *Don't run water under the hay.*

If your actions are not transparent and open, it creates mistrust or doubt from others. Be honorable and avoid secret schemes, because people eventually will not trust you.

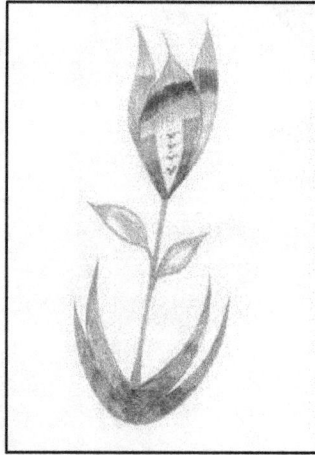

مار هم په دښمن وژنه.

Maar ham pa dukhman wazhna.

Literal: *Better to let your enemy kill the snake.*

If you have two enemies, let them fight each other first if you can. Then only one will be left for you to fight. If you choose to fight first, then you will have to defeat two enemies at once.

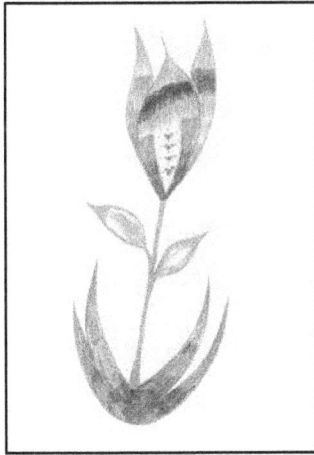

له زړه نه بل زړه ته لار شته.

La zra na bal zra ta laar shta.

Literal: *From one heart to another, there is a way.*

When two people have the same intent and feel close to each
other, they will find a way to succeed on the same path.

Also: Said when two people meet by chance
and want to keep in touch with each other.

هم د زړه کیږی، هم د ساړه کیږی.

Hum da zra kaigee, hum da saara kaigee.

Literal: *While the heart desires, the feelings are cold.*

To be indecisive, or to be of two minds about something.

Also: When a person has an intense urge to act, but a certain feeling or intuition inside says to be careful.

English equivalent: "To have cold feet."

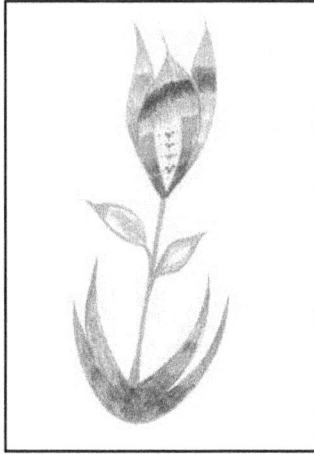

تور ي ته ګنډي نيسه، خبرو ته تنډي نيسه.

Toree ta gandee neesa, khabaro ta tandee neesa.

Literal: *Use a sword against a shield,*
and a bold front against words.

A person should use the appropriate weapon in any type of
conflict. Stand your ground with dignity and
honor, and do not overreact.

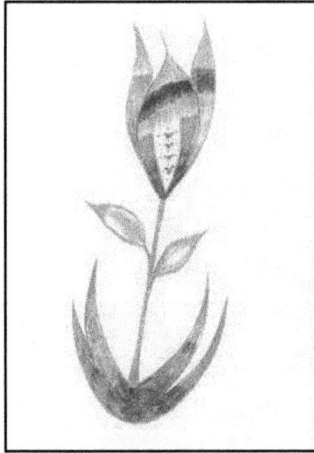

تورې په لالا وهي مړی په عبدالله وهي.

Tooray ba Lala wahee nwarey maray ba Abdullah wahee.

Literal: *Lala accomplishes feats while Abdullah eats.*

When one person does all the work, but the rewards or benefits go to someone who contributes nothing.

كار په كولو كيږي.

Kaar pa kawalo kegi.

Literal: The work gets done by doing it.

Good things happen with good effort. Ideas, plans and conversation are useful, but nothing happens without action.

English equivalent:
"When the going gets tough, the tough get going."

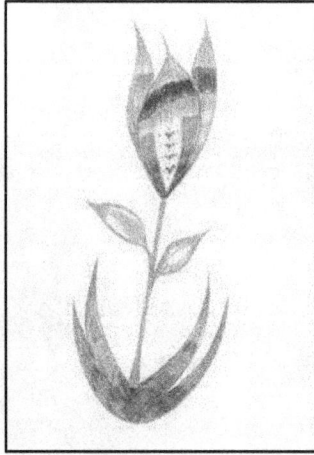

د دروغو مزل لنډ وي.

Da drogho mazal land we.

Literal: *Lies cannot be hidden for long.*

Lies and dishonesty are almost always exposed in the end.
Something that is built on lies cannot endure.

English equivalent: "The truth will out."

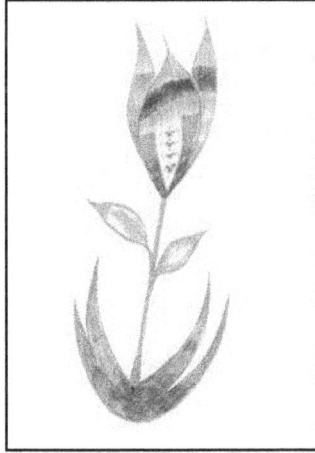

توکڼۍ لاڼي بيا خُلي ته نه راځي.

Tokali laari bya khuli ta na razee.

Literal: *Spit once spat does not return to the mouth.*

Think very carefully before you do or say certain things,
because some things cannot be undone.

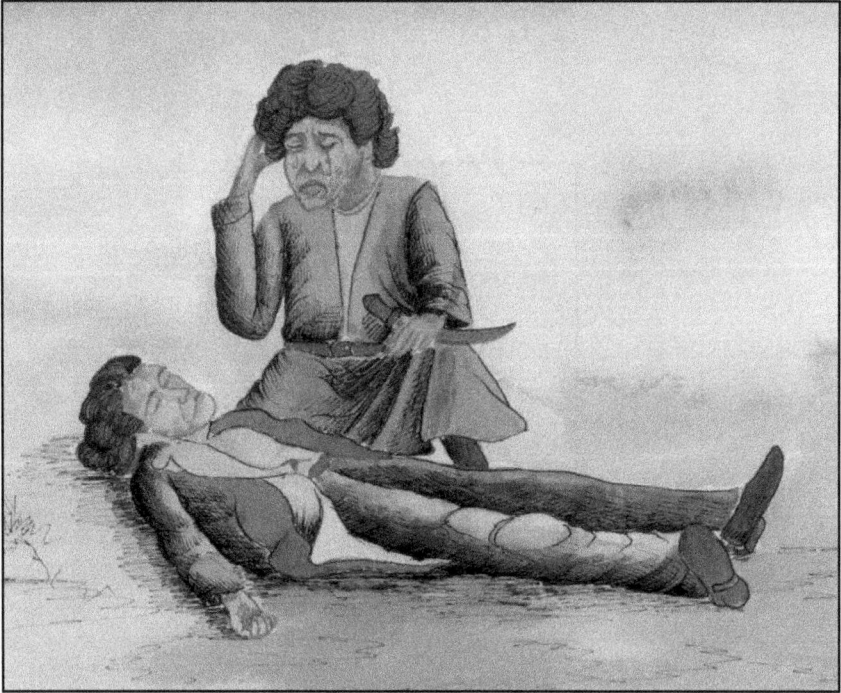

کور کلی په زور نه کیږي.

Kor kalay pa zor na kegi.

Literal: *Community cannot be created by force.*

True and healthy relationships are built by mutual choice and respect, not by force. You cannot force someone to like you or cooperate with you, even if it seems to work in the short term.

English equivalent:
"You can catch more flies with honey than you can with vinegar."

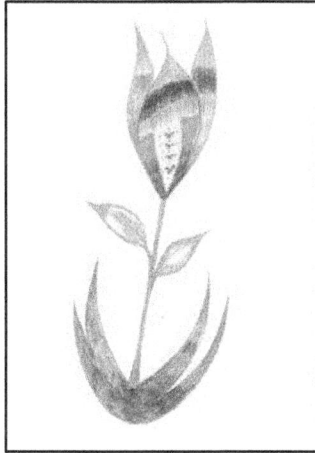

په پوښتنه سړی مکې ته رسیږي.

Pa pohtana saray makee ta rasege.

Literal: *By asking, a person can get all the way to Mecca.*

If you have a need or a question, it is important to speak up.
If you don't, people will not know that you need help.

English equivalent: "The squeaky wheel gets the grease"

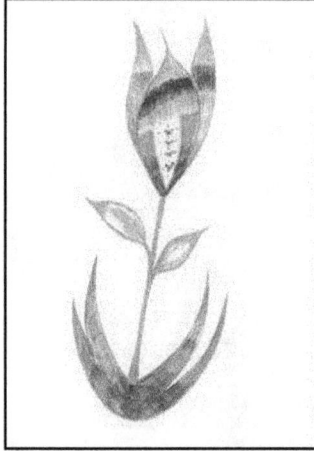

غر په غر نه ورځي،
خو بنده په بنده ورځي.

Ghar pa ghar na warzi, kho banda pa banda warzi.

Literal: *Mountains do not draw*
nearer to each other, but people do.

It is important to recognize that all people are fellow humans.
If people cooperate, are fair with each other, and are willing to
compromise, they can solve most problems or disputes.

دلته دم او قدم دواړه په حساب دي.

Dalta dam aw qadam dwarra pa hesab de.

Literal: *Here the steps and the moment are being counted.*

Everything you do or say matters, even when you think no one is watching. God sees everything, and holds people accountable for their words, thoughts and actions.

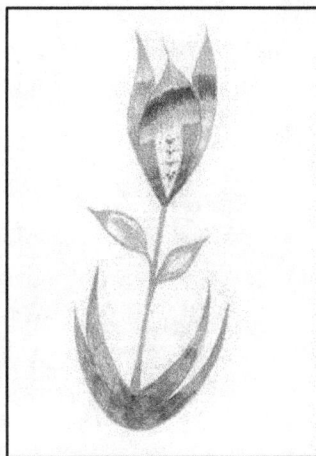

پاروگر د مار له لاسه مري.

Parhogar da mar la lasa mrey.

Literal: *A snake charmer is finally dying due to the snake.*

Said when a person is hurt by someone whom he loves, or is injured when doing something that he enjoys.

English equivalent: "To bite the hand that feeds you."

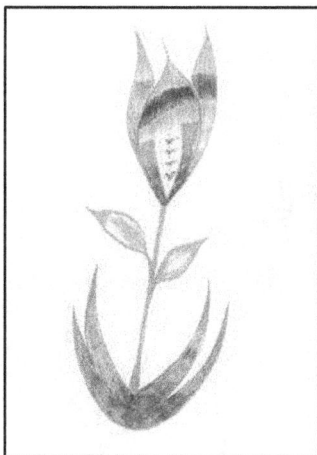

د طاقت نه مهارت ښه دی.

Da taqat na mahaarat kha di.

Literal: Skill is better than power.

It usually is better to act with elegance and finesse rather
than to rely on blunt force or influence. To be clever and
intelligent is better than to have only brute strength.

هر څوک پوزه توره
کړي چې زه لوهار يم.

Har sok poza tora kre che za lohaar yum.

Literal: *Everybody blackens their nose*
to claim they are a blacksmith.

Be careful of judging people by their appearance, their boasts,
or their unproven claims of expertise. Some people try to
pose as experts when they actually know very little.

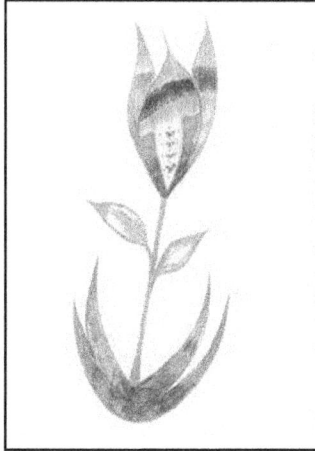

ميرزي هم په خپل کور مست وي.

Meezhay ham pa khpal koor masst we.

Literal: *An ant has power in his home.*

An ant might be very small and regularly gets stepped
on in the outside world, but inside his own anthill he
has authority and status. People are the same way,
and this power at home should not be abused.

English equivalent: *"A man's home is his castle."*

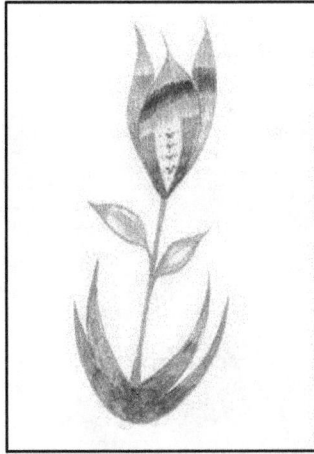

دوه هیندوانۍ په یو لاس کی نه نیول کیږی.

Dwa hendwany pa yewa laas ki na newal kegy.

Literal: *You can't carry two watermelons in one hand.*

Don't take on more than you can handle,
or attempt what is impossible.

English equivalent: "Don't bite off more than you can chew."

عقل د کم عقلو نه زده کیږی.

Aqal da kam aqlo na zda kezhy.

Literal: *Wisdom can be learned from those who don't have it.*

Be observant, and learn from foolish mistakes that
others make. You can learn just as much from
bad examples as you can from good ones.

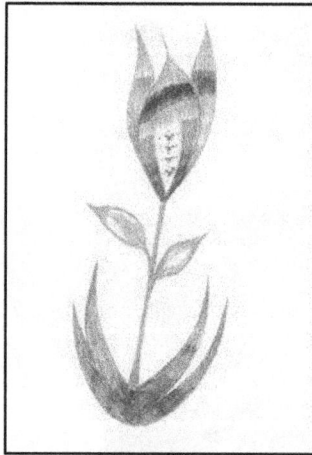

زمری ته خدای په هر ځای
کی غوښه ورکوی.

Zmaray ta khudai pa har zay ke ghwakha warkawi.

Literal: *God provides the lion with meat wherever he is.*

Don't worry too much about anything. If you are brave and righteous, God will surely give you what you really need.

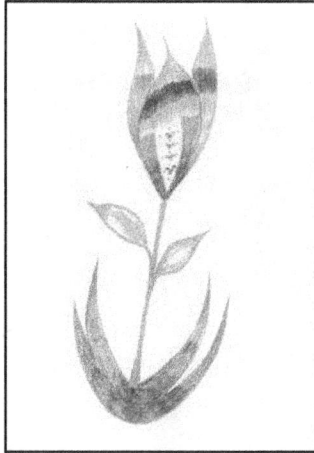

خپل عمل د لارې مل دي.

Khpal amal da laarey mal dy.

Literal: *Your own actions guard you on your journey.*

Every person is responsible for his own actions. If your deeds are good, you will be rewarded in this life or the next. If you do bad things, sooner or later you will pay a price.

انسان تر کاڼي کلک دی
او تر ګل نازک دی.

Ensaan tar kanhe kalak aw tar gul nazak dai.

Literal: *A human is strong as a stone and as delicate as a flower.*

Even though people can endure almost anything, sometimes they can become emotional, sad or hurt over something small.

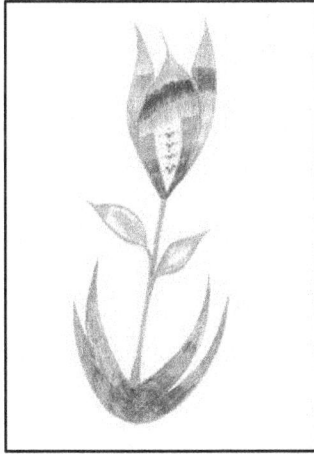

میږي ته چې خدای په قهر شي نو وزرې ورکوي.

Megi ta che Khoday pa qahr shi no wazare warkawi.

Literal: *When God wants to punish ants, he gives them wings.*

Sometimes people suffer when they have power and "blessings" that do not match their true natures.

(*Note:* Some ants grow wings shortly before they die.)

English equivalent: "Both a blessing and a curse."

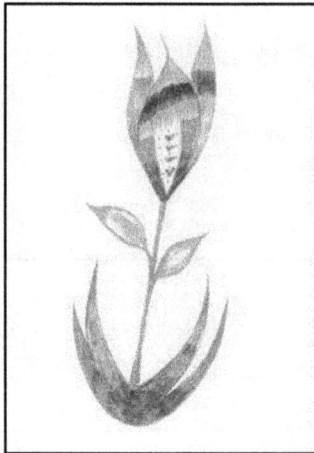

علم د بنه سرري نه ډېر بنه او
د بد سرري نه ډېر بد جوړوي.

Elam da ha sarri na der ha aw
da bad sarri na der bad jorrawi.

Literal: *Knowledge makes a good man better, and a bad man worse.*

Education creates strengths that can be used for good or evil,
depending on the nature of the person who receives it.

English equivalent: "Knowledge is power."

خپل څادر سره پښي غځوه.

Khpal saadar sara pkhi ghazawah.

Literal: *Spread your feet in keeping with your chador.*

Don't take on more than you can handle. Don't overstretch your spending, or borrow beyond what you can afford.

English equivalent: "Don't bite off more than you can chew."

(*Note:* A *chador* is a long, billowing garment or cloak that exposes a woman's face but covers her head and body.)

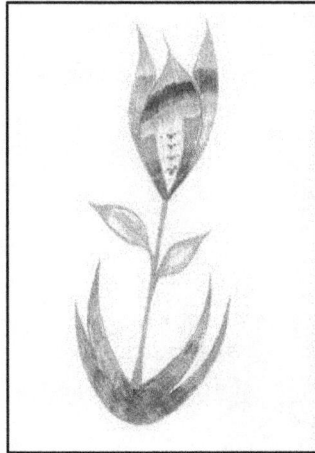

بیکارو ته شیطان کار پیدا کوی.

Bekaru ta shaitan kar paida kawi.

Literal: An idler's brain is the devil's workshop.

People without meaningful things to keep them busy
often find trouble to fill their time instead.

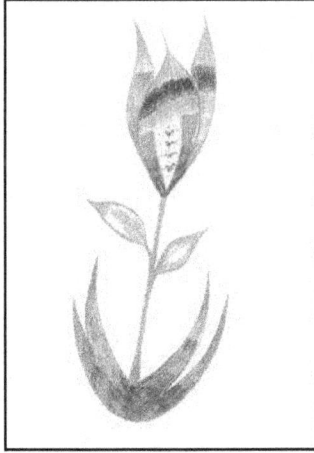

خواړه د ښبنتن پخيږي
او ملا د وينځي کږيږي.

Khwaara da sehtan pakhigi au mlaa de winze kagigi.

Literal: *The master's food is being cooked,*
and the servant's back is becoming crooked.

Wealthy or influential people enjoy the amenities of life and
profit from the hard work of others, who sometimes
pay a physical price for their labors.

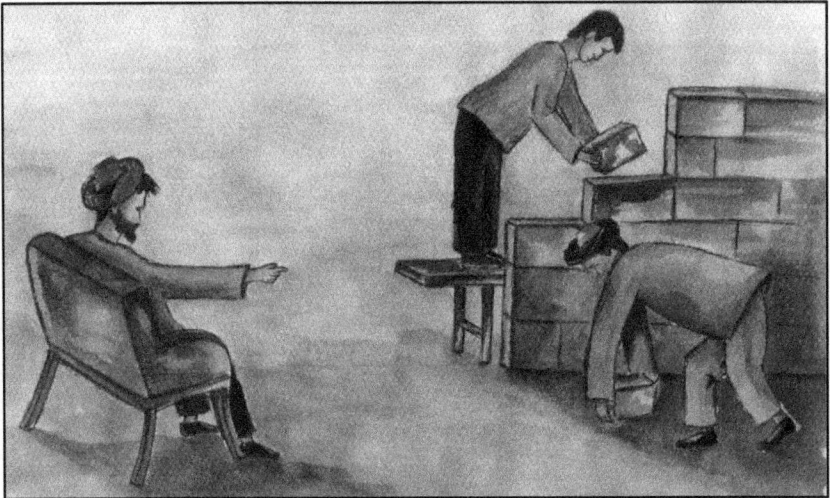

د نر زوي ژړا په زانګو
کښي معلومېږي.

Da nar zooy zharaa pah zaangu ke maaloomaygee.

Literal: The cry of a brave child is heard in the crib.

Strong and courageous people have unique characters. Their true personalities can be seen even in early childhood.

English equivalent: "The child is father of the man"

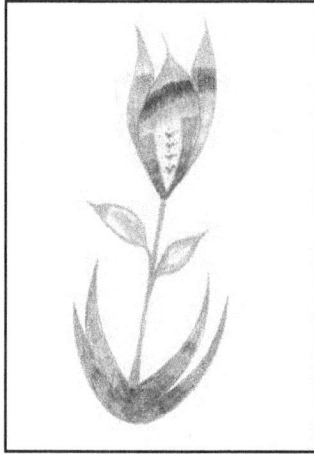

راست اوسه په سمه
لار کښې ملاست اوسه.

Raast osa pa sama laar ki mlaast osa.

Literal: *Stay on course and keep resting on the right path.*

The right path also is an emotionally restful path.
If your intentions are good and your actions are noble,
then you have nothing to fear or worry about.
Your good path will safeguard you on your way.

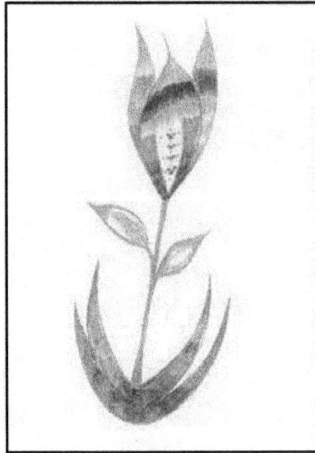

تللی وخت بیرته په لاس نه راځي.

Tlalai wakht berta pa laas na razi.

Literal: The past is not coming back.

A person cannot go back in time to do something over again.
What is done is done, so don't dwell on it.

هوښياره مرغۍ د دواړو پښو نه نخلي.

Okhyaara marghay da dwaaro pkho na nkhaley.

Literal: *The clever bird gets both feet trapped.*

Clever people are hard to catch, but if they
are outsmarted it can be hard for them to escape.

Also: Used in ironic situations where
an otherwise intelligent person fails a simple task.

English equivalent: *"Too smart for his own good."*

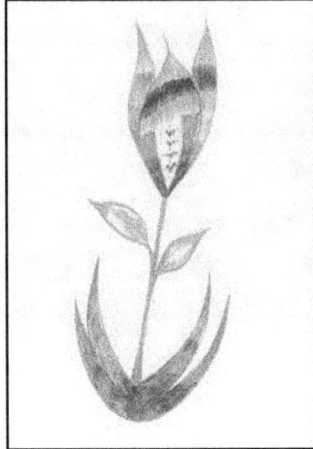

بار چه خر نه وړي
نو په خپله به ئي وړي.

Bar che khar na wre no pa khpala ba yee wrey.

Literal: *You will have to carry the load if the donkey won't carry it.*

It is important to be self-reliant and not overly dependent
on others. Some things have to be done
even if there is no one to help you.

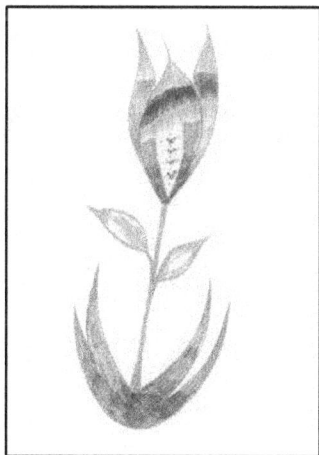

شتمنه بنځه به درنه غلام جوړوي.

Shtamana khaza ba derna ghulaam jorrawi.

Literal: *A rich wife will make you a slave.*

If you gain something without working for it,
you will end up paying for it somehow in the end.

پیسه د لاس خیری ده.

Paisa de laas khiray da.

Literal: *Money is the dirt on your hands.*

Money and material wealth do not endure,
and are not the most important things in life.

(*Note*: Money is earned through work, but you spend it after
you earn it. This is like getting your hands dirty in a day of
hard work, then washing off the dirt in the evening.)

English equivalent: "You can't take it with you."

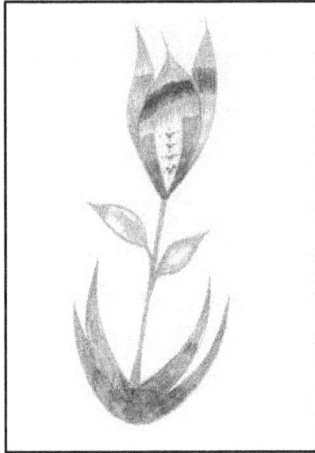

میږونه مري خو نومونه یي پاتي کیږي.

Mahroona marhee kho nomona eh pah-ta-kee-jhee.

Literal: *The brave die, but their legends remain forever.*

It is important to show courage and dignity in the
face of adversity or danger. People will remember
your acts as a good example to follow.

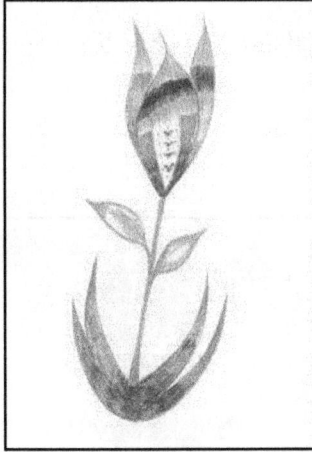

تلَه د چا مخ نه کوي.

Talah da cha makh na kawee.

Literal: *A weighing scale does not favor anyone.*

Sometimes the facts are the facts, and you cannot escape them.
They cannot be changed by wishing, favoritism or influence.

چي روپۍ وي بركي چیلی ډیرې.

Che rupay we braggi chailai derey.

Literal: If you have money, there are many two-colored goats.

Money can buy any form of luxury and satisfy every
material whim, no matter how strange or rare.

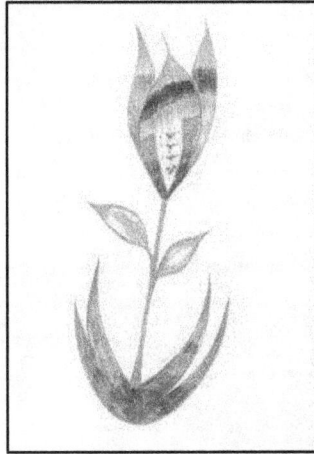

د باران نه تښتتیدم،
د ناوي لاندي مي شپه شوه.

Da baraan na tahtedam, da naway landay mee shpah shwah.

Literal: I escaped from the rain but stood under a rain gutter.

Be careful that your actions to avoid something
do not put you in an even worse position.

English equivalent: "Out of the frying pan and into the fire."

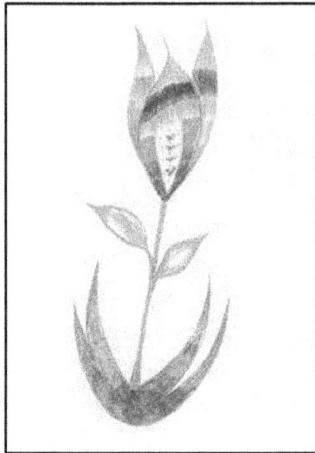

اول شوق وي بيا چتي شي.

Awal shawq we byaa chatti she.

Literal: First there is interest, then it becomes an addiction.

People often pursue pleasures out of curiosity and enjoy them at first. But if they are not careful, they can lose control and gradually be enslaved by pleasure - or even destroyed by it.

د کبرکاسه نسکوره ده.

Da kabar kasa naskoora da.

Literal: The bowl of arrogance always ends upside down.

If people are too haughty or prideful they eventually will fail.
It is better to behave with modesty and humility,
and let your actions speak for themselves.

English equivalent: "Pride goes before a fall."

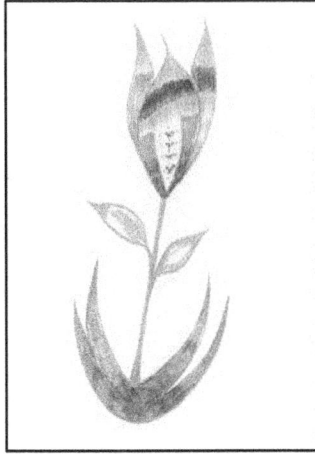

بل ته يوه ګوته نيول
حُان ته څلور ګوتي نيول دي.

Bal ta yewa gota newal zaan ta salor gwatee newal di.

Literal: *To point one finger at someone else*
points four fingers at yourself.

Be careful about blaming others for your own problems.
You should consider that the fault may be your own.

English equivalent: "Those who live in glass houses
shouldn't throw stones."

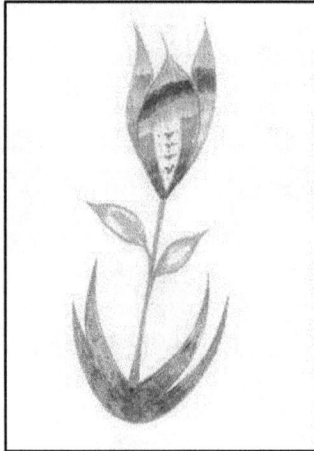

لـه يوه لاس نـه تـک نـه خيـُي.

La yawa laas na tak na khezhi.

Literal: *You cannot clap with one hand.*

Just as one hand cannot clap by itself, a person
rarely can succeed alone. Cooperating
with others achieves a better effect.

Also: Before blaming a single person, one should
consider the possible involvement of others.

English equivalent: "No man is an island."

چیندخه په لوته وختله
ویل یې چې کشمیر مې ولید.

Chindakha pa luta wokhatala
wayel ye che kashmir me wolid.

Literal: *A frog climbed on a cloud*
and claimed to have seen Kashmir.

Some people exaggerate and boast to have done things that
are impossible for them to do. They claim that they have
seen, done and achieved the best - even if it is not true.

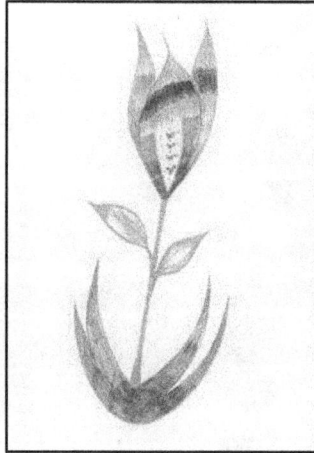

که شپه تیاره ده خو منۍ په شمار دي.

Ka shpa tyarah da kho manri pah shmaar de.

Literal: *Even if the night is dark, the apples have been counted.*

Do not despair in the midst of injustice,
because the result will be fair in the end.

(*Note*: Although some people may seem to "get away with
things" at the expense of others, all people ultimately
will be held accountable in this life or the next.)

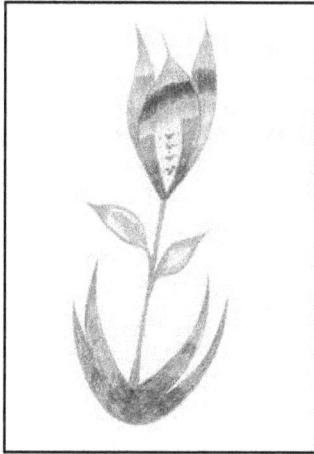

ترکانی د بیزو کار نه دي.

Tarkani de beezo kar na de.

Literal: Carpentry is not monkey's business.

Things that require expertise, precision or skill
are better left to people who have those qualities.

کاڼی به پوست نه شي
او دښمن به دوست نه شي.

Kaanay ba post na shi aw dokhman ba dost na shi.

Literal: *A stone will never be soft and an enemy never a friend.*

A true enemy will never change his real attitude toward you, so be very careful about trusting his intentions.

English equivalent: "A leopard can't change its spots."

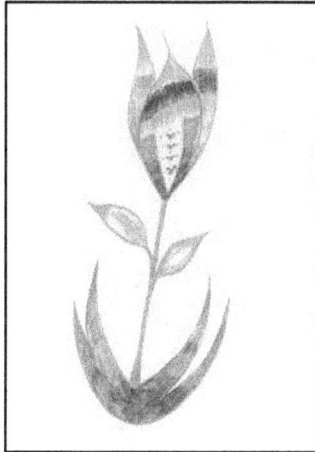

پہ تورہ مر شی نہ چی دښمن تہ خر شی.

Pa toora mar she na chee dukhman ta kher she.

Literal: *Better killed by a sword than defiled by an enemy.*

Reflects part of the Pashtun code of honor known as
Pashtunwali. Some other elements of this unwritten code
include hospitality, asylum, revenge, loyalty, bravery, justice,
love of God and nation, and protecting the honor of women.

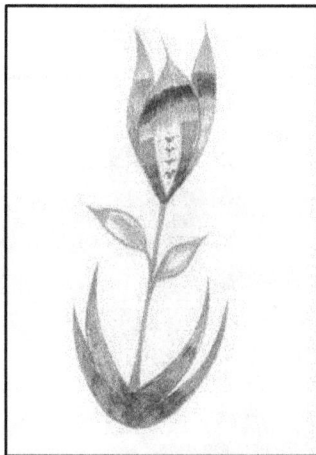

عزت کوه عزت به دې کیږي.

Ezat kawa ezat ba de kegi.

Literal: *Respect others in order to be respected.*

True respect cannot be forced, it must be earned.
A person who is worthy of respect gains it by
treating others politely and respectfully too.

English equivalent:
"Do unto others as you would have them do unto you."

اول وخوره د خُان غوبنی،
بیا وخوره د ښکار غوبنی

Awal wakhrah da zaan ghwakhi,
bya wakhrah da khkaar ghwakhi.

Literal: *First eat your own meat, then eat hunted meat.*

Try hard to learn things, develop expertise, and become
skilled and self-reliant. Then you can achieve your
goals and enjoy the fruits of your earlier labors.

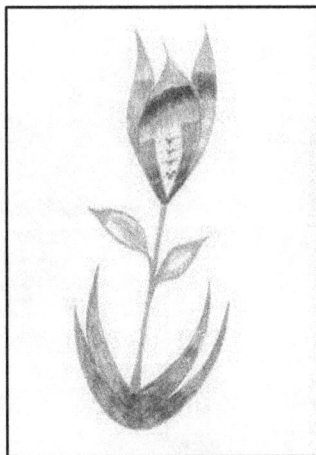

چی غل نه یی له پاچا هم مه ویریږه.

Che ghal na yee la pacha hm ma werezha.

Literal: If you are not a thief fear no one, even a king.

If you are good, honest and trustworthy in your
thoughts and actions, you do not need to be
afraid of anyone or anything in this world.

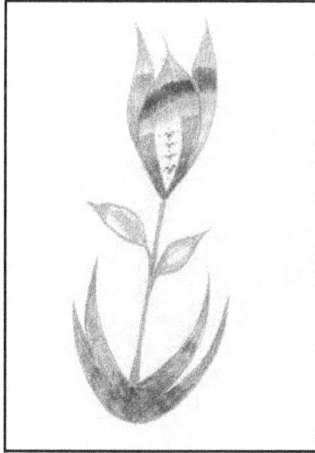

په يو ګل نه پسرلی کيږي.

Pa yau gul na pesarlay kigi.

Literal: *One flower does not make spring.*

Change and progress requires cooperation and teamwork.
It is hard for one person to accomplish a big project
or improve an entire situation by himself or herself.

آسمان ته د ختو لار نشته.

Asmaan ta da khato laar nashta.

Literal: *There is no path climbing up to the sky.*

There are no shortcuts in life. Don't run after impossible or impractical things. Wishful thinking and glamorous conversations alone do not achieve goals. Think big and take action, but also stay grounded in reality.

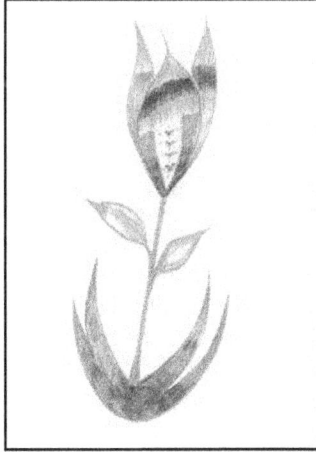

کَه غر لوړدی پَه سر لارلري.

Kha ghar lwar day pa sar laar lary.

Literal: Even if a mountain is very high, there is a path to the top.

Nothing is impossible - there is always a way. There is no problem without a solution, even if the problem seems impossible to solve at first glance.

With hope, effort and creativity, there is always a way to overcome difficult situations and succeed.

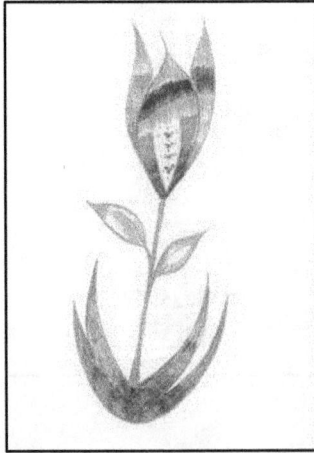

پیشو په خوب کښي غوښي ویني.

Pisho pa khob ke ghwakhi wenee.

Literal: *A cat sees meat in its dreams.*

Sometimes a person becomes obsessed with one thing
above all else. This Matal describes people who only
pursue their own interests and passions, and are
unable to focus on other worthwhile things.

م زر ما او تول زما.

Meem zarr maa aow toll zma.

Literal: *When things come to me, they are all mine.*

An ironic Matal that means a person
should not be greedy or selfish.

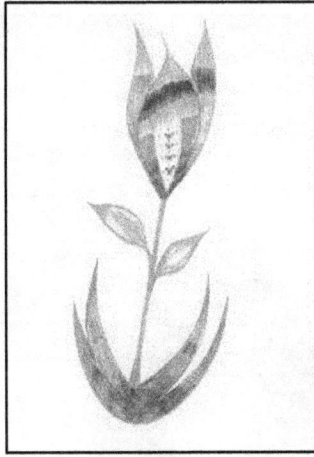

چې څه تیار وي هغه د یار وي.

Che sa tayaar we hagha da yaar we.

Literal: For my friend, whatever is ready.

Hospitality is an obligation for every Afghan household. Even a guest who arrives on short notice should be served the best that is available.

Also: A person should extend every kind of help possible to assist a friend.

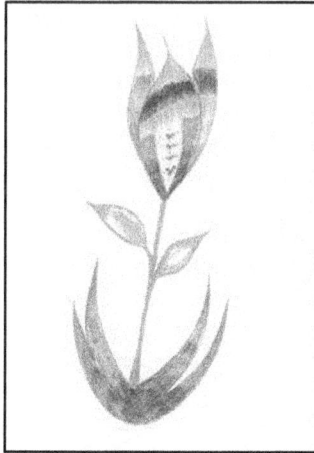

د ورو کار نه وي خو اوزگار هم نه وي.

Da waro kaar na we kho oozgar ham na we.

Literal: Children have no occupations, but they are not idle either.

Although children have no big responsibilities, they are never wasting time when they are exploring things or playing. Even if these activities seem directionless, children learn from everything they do and all they experience.

پر می کره نو مر می کره.

Parr may kra no marr may kra.

Literal: *If proven guilty, I will accept death.*

An open challenge often said in arguments by people
who are 100% confident that they are right or innocent.

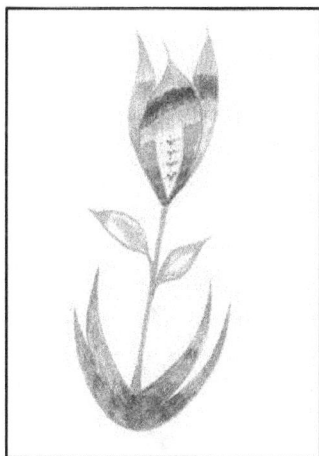

اصیل ته اشارت کم اصل ته کوتک.

Aseel tah isharat kamasal ta kotak.

Literal: *A nod to the noble person and a rod for the foolish.*

An educated or smart person can be taught easily,
but it is harder for the ignorant or ill-bred to learn
without something specific to motivate them.

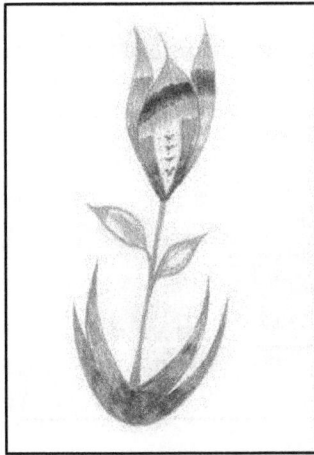

مه کوه په چا چي وبه شي په تا.

Ma kawa pa chaa che wobashi pa taa.

Literal: *Do not do to others what you would not have done to you.*

Don't do harm to others, because eventually
you will pay a price yourself.

English equivalent is also known as the Golden Rule:
"Do unto others as you would have done unto you."

اوبنان چی ساتی،
دروازی به دنگی جوړوی.

Ukhan che saate, darwaze ba dangy jorawy.

If you keep camels, make your doors high.

If you intend to do something big,
make sure you have a plan and prepare for it.

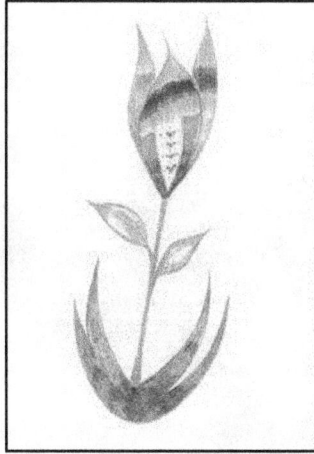

چي بد ګرځي بد به پرځي.

Che bad garzee bad ba parzee.

Literal: *Bad company will have a bad outcome.*

People can be judged by their associates. If you spend time with bad people you will become even more like them, and it probably will not end well.

English equivalent: *"Birds of a feather flock together."*

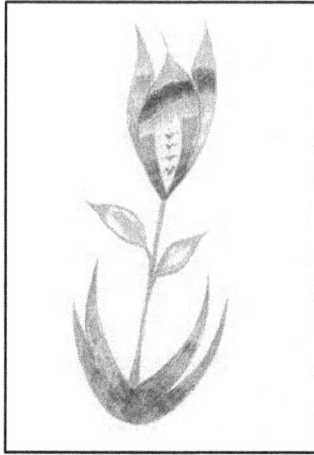

وخت د هر غم دوا دی.

Wakht da har gham dawa dy.

Literal: *Time is the medicine for all sadness.*

Even the greatest heartaches will have
some relief with the passage of time.

English equivalent: "Time heals all wounds."

بنده حیران خدای پر مهربان.

Bandah heraan khuday par mehrabaan.

Literal: *Man marvels at God's kindness.*

Life is a gift. God blesses us with so much that sometimes
we forget to appreciate it. If we are content and thankful
for these blessings, we will be rewarded with even more.

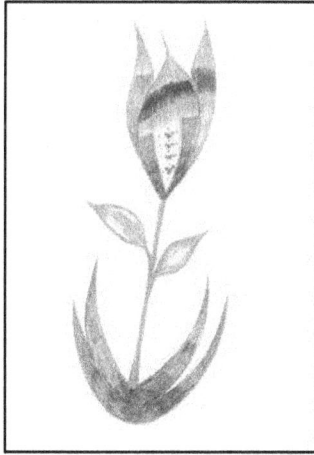

بنه وکړه ، دریاب ته یې واچوه.

Kha wakrha, daryab ta ye wachawa.

Literal: *Do virtue and throw it in the river.*

A person should not do good deeds expecting rewards
or praise, but rather should do them for their own sake.
Do virtuous things quietly and then forget about it.
In the end, you will receive rewards anyway.

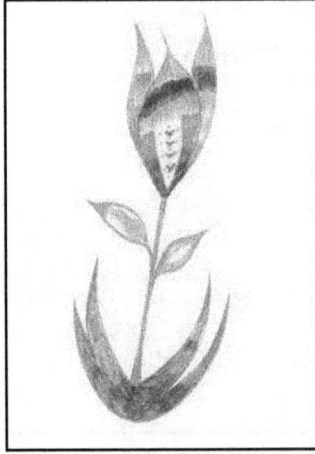

خپله ژبه هم کلا ده هم بلا.

Khpala zhaba ham kalaa da ham balaa.

Literal: *Your tongue is either castle or calamity.*

What you say, how you say it, and when you say it
can help you. But words also can get you in big trouble,
so choose carefully what you say. Words have
meaning, and people remember them.

تر ورخه تیری اوبه بیرته نه راګرځی.

Tar warkha teere uba berta na ragarzy.

Literal: *Water that has passed through a sluice cannot return back.*

Some decisions or actions cannot be undone.

English equivalent: *"It's water under the bridge."*

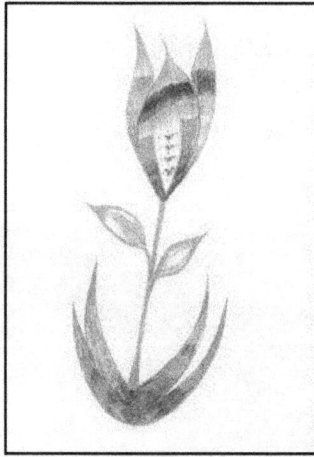

پردې کټ تر نیمو شپو وي.

Praday kat tar nemo shpo we.

Literal: A borrowed bed is only until midnight.

It is better to be self-reliant and independent rather than to
count on the charity of others. You cannot feel secure
if you rely too much on other people or their things,
because they always could be taken away.

Also: If you borrow something you should return it whenever
the owner wants it back, even if it is inconvenient for you.

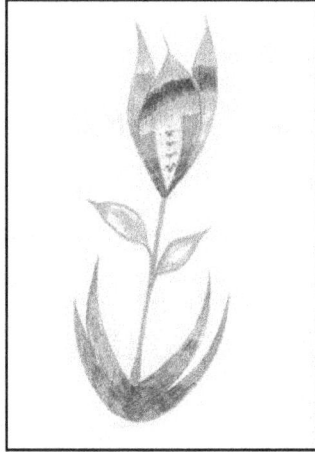

د سوال په اوبو ژرنده نه ګرځي.

Da swaal pa obo zhrandah na garzee.

Literal: *A watermill cannot run on borrowed water.*

Living by borrowing or counting too much on the
goodwill of others is not wise, sustainable, or good business.

دنیا د ارت لوتکي ده.

Doonya da art lotakay da.

Literal: *The world is like buckets on a waterwheel.*

The waterwheel in this classic Matal represents the cycle of life
and eternity. People come and go, but life goes on. When
people are born they have nothing, and they leave
the world with nothing.

(*Note:* In rural parts of Afghanistan, some water wells
use a wheel with many buckets attached to it. Each
bucket scoops up water as the wheel turns, and then
empties into a larger bucket at the end of the cycle.)

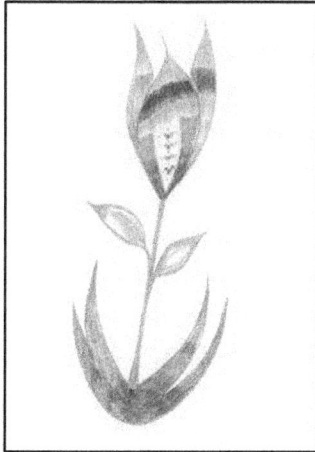

مطلبي په خټه اور لګوي.

Matlabee pah khatta aor lagawee.

Literal: *A selfish person tries to set mud on fire.*

Selfish people are obsessed with following their own
desires, no matter how impractical. They will not listen to
the advice of others who know better - for example,
when they are told that mud does not burn.

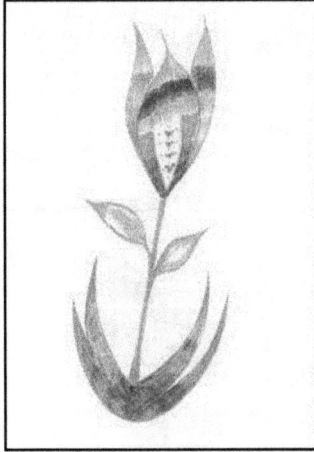

لمدو ختو ته لږي اوبه بهانه وي.

Lamdo khato ta lagee oba bahaana we.

Literal: *Adding a little water to wet mud is the cause.*

Sometimes a tense standoff will explode because of one small act that creates a much bigger problem. Generally used in the context of a volatile situation.

English equivalents: "Adding fuel to the fire," "Waking a sleeping giant," and "The straw that broke the camel's back."

په ګڼو قصابانو کښې غوا مرداريږي.

Pah ganrro qasabano ki ghwa murdaaregey.

Literal: *Too many butchers ruin the meat.*

When too many people get involved in managing a
project, it can be harder to achieve success.

English equivalent: *"Too many cooks spoil the soup."*

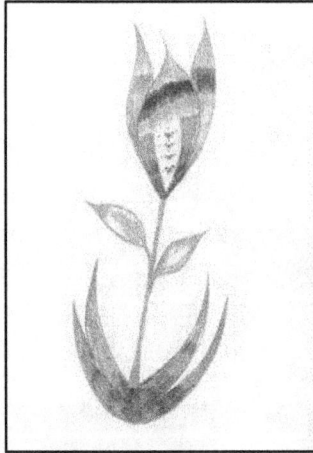

پـه يـو تـيـكي كـښـې دوه تـورې نـه ځـائـيـږي.

Pah yow tekey ki dwah tooray na zayegee.

Literal: You cannot fit two swords in one sheath.

It is impossible for two kings to rule one land. It also can be hard for two powerful forces to work together.

Also: A person cannot serve two masters.

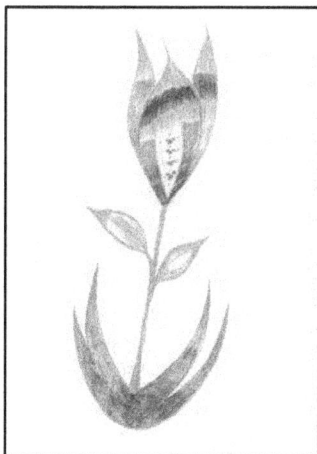

چي څومره غټ وي دومره لټ وي.

Che sumra ghat we dumra lat we.

Literal: *The fatter a person is, the lazier he is.*

In Afghan culture, it is a widely held belief that lazy people become fat because they are not as physically active.

د ړندو په ښار کې يو سترگی پاچا وي.

De randoo pa haar ke yaw stargay paachaa wey.

Literal: *Among the blind, a one-eyed man is king.*

No person knows everything, or is perfectly wise.
But even a little bit of knowledge or wisdom is
much better than none at all.

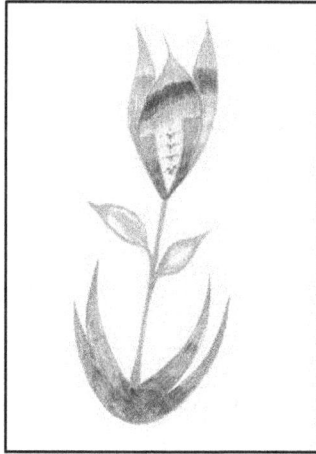

د خره مينه لغته ده.

Da khra mina laghata da.

Literal: Donkeys show their love by kicking you.

This Matal refers to a person who is too unmannered
or immature to show his affection properly, even if he
likes or loves someone. So instead, he stupidly tries to
provoke or hurt the object of his affection.

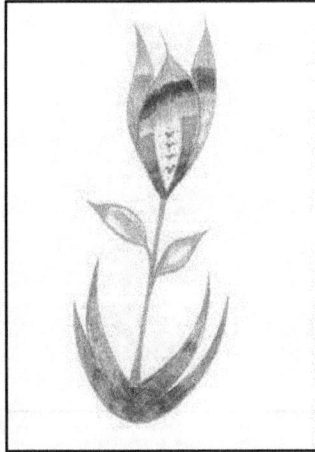

د قسمت ليک نه نوريزي.

Da qismat leek na noregey.

Literal: *What is written in fate cannot be changed.*

Fate is preordained. People can affect individual events,
but they cannot influence the master plan. The ultimate
destiny of a person or thing cannot be changed.

خاثكى، خاثكى نه سمندر جوړيږی.

Saske, saske, na samandar jorhege.

Literal: An ocean is made drop by drop.

The small contributions and teamwork of ordinary individuals can produce a big result. Small works are not necessarily less important, and can add up to greater things.

Also: Don't give up – good things take time and patience.

English equivalent: "Slow and steady wins the race."

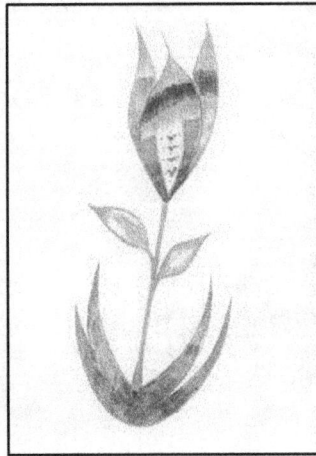

چي غل نه تښتي، نو مل دي وتښتي.

Chee ghal na tahti, no mal de wotehti.

Literal: *If a thief doesn't want to flee, friends should flee.*

If someone ignores your good advice to do or not do something, then eventually you should stop trying to convince him and look after your own best interests.

Also: If a bad person does not run away when he is discovered, he may be dangerous and determined to fight. You and your friends should consider leaving the scene unless you are ready to fight too.

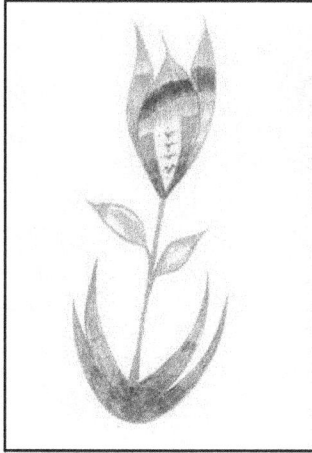

چي سر وي توپۍ ډېرۍ.

Che sar we topai deray.

Literal: *If there's a head there are plenty of hats.*

The world is full of opportunities. Don't worry about any single loss too much, because you are still alive to make other gains. Your life and health are far more valuable than any amount of gold or money.

English equivalent: "Live to fight another day."

مارته په لستوني کبنی ځای مه ورکوه.

Mar taa parlastooney kee zai mah warkawa.

Literal: Don't let a snake live in your sleeve.

Keep a distance from your enemies whenever
you can. Don't allow them easy access to
valuable things if you can help it.

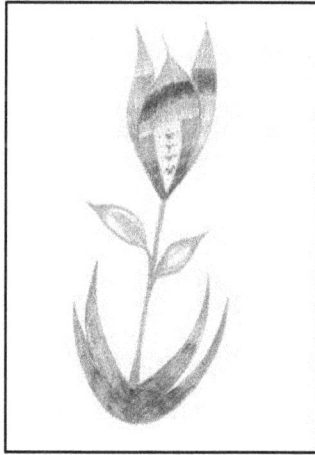

ثنكه غر هغسي ځناور.

Sanga ghar haghasi zanaawar.

Literal: *Each type of mountain has its own kind of animal.*

Every environment shapes the character of the creatures that live in it. This is true for all living things.

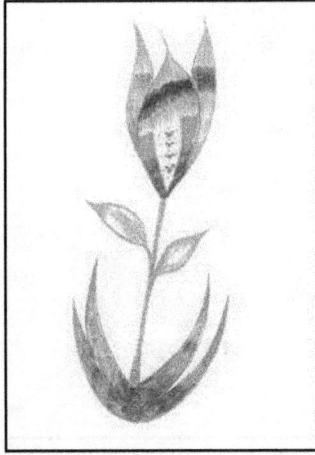

له پیښی نه تیښته نشته.

Lah paikhey na tekhta nishta.

Literal: *You cannot run from your fate.*

A person's destiny is decided before birth, and only God can change it. There is no way to escape or hide from this.

English equivalent: "Whatever will be, will be."

د یوې سپږې لپاره
ټول پوستین په اور مه سوځه.

Da yawe spage lapara
tol posteen pah owr mah swazah.

Literal: Don't burn a whole overcoat for just a flea.

Do not destroy or reject something valuable
because of a single small mistake or flaw.

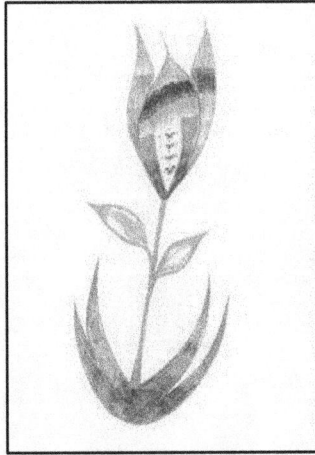

خپل بد د ولو مينځ وي.

Khpal bad da welo myanz we.

Literal: *Our own fault is like a flaw between our shoulder blades.*

Some people are quick to point out the defects and mistakes of others but cannot see their own, just as a person cannot see his own back between the shoulder blades.

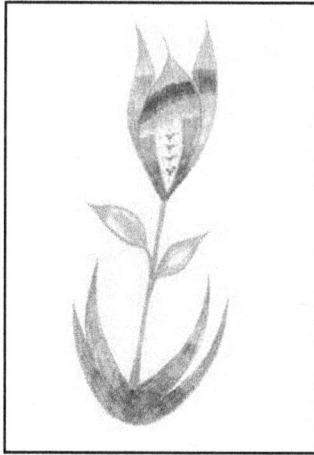

چي اوږه نه خوري بوي ترې نه ځي.

Che ooga na khuray boey tre na zee.

Literal: *You won't smell like garlic if you don't eat it.*

People judge the character of others by what they do and who
their friends are. Stay away from bad things and bad people,
and you will keep a good and honorable reputation.

چې په خوی سره ثاني وي
د هغو سره ياري وي.

Che pa khoy sara saanee we da hagho sara yaaree we.

Literal: If personalities match, friendships develop.

People who are of like mind or compatible personalities tend
to get along well together and enjoy each other's company.

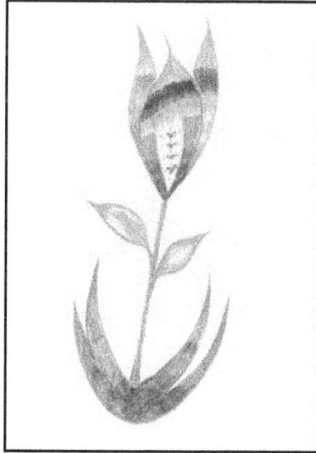

چې په گُړه مري
زهرو ته حاجت نشته.

Che pa gurrah mree zahro ta haajat nashta.

Literal: If you can kill by using gur (a lump of sugar)
there is no need to use poison.

You do not always have to use extreme measures to solve a
problem. Look for easier, simpler or more elegant ways.

English equivalent:
"You can catch more flies with honey than you can with vinegar."

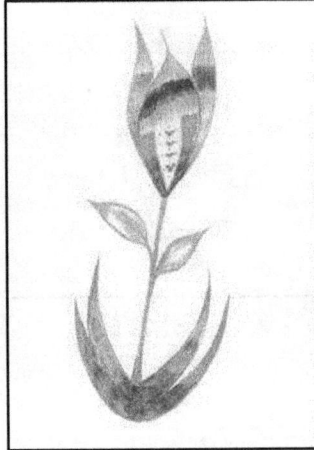

طبيب هغه چې په ځان ئې تير وي.

Tabeeb hagha che pa zaan yi ter we.

Literal: The best healer is one who has been healed.

Experience is important and helps a person to truly
understand things. Wise people listen to advice
from those who are more experienced.

پہ پردي لاس مار وژل هم بنه نه دي.

Pah pradey laas maar wazhal ham kha na de.

Literal: It isn't good to get a snake killed by another's hand.

Don't rely too much on other people. It is better to do something yourself than to count on someone else to do it. Don't let someone else do your dirty work for you.

Also: There is no harm in getting advice from wise people, but in the end one must act upon one's own plans.

English equivalent: "Self done is well done."

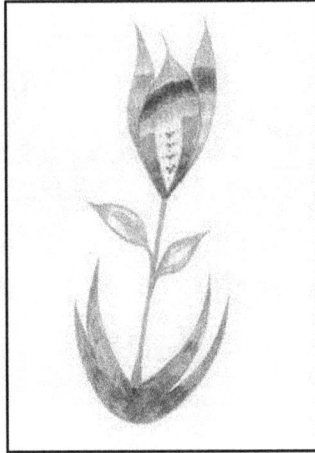

كه بنوال بڼ لري، چغال هم خداى لري.

Kah banwal bann larey, chaghal ham khuday larey.

Literal: *If a gardener has his garden, the jackal also has God.*

A rich person may have many material things, but a poor person still has God - which is infinitely more important.

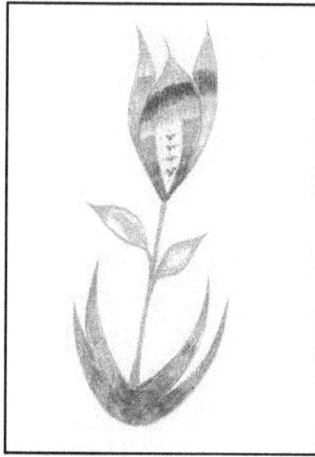

غم او بنادي خور او ورور دي.

Gham aow haadey khor ao wror dee.

Literal: Sorrow and joy are sisters and brothers.

Happiness and sadness are part of life,
and they are related to each other.

هر چا ته خپل وطن کشمیر دي.

Har cha ta khpal watan Kashmir de.

Literal: *Everyone's homeland is like Kashmir to them.*

Kashmir (a region between India and Pakistan) is considered by Afghans to be a beautiful and wonderful place. All people have a natural attachment to their homeland.

(Note: Many Afghans consider Kashmir to be one of the most beautiful places in Asia.)

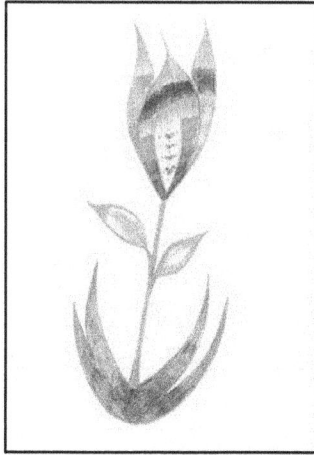

وطن هغه چي تن په کښي خوشحاله وي.

Watan hagha che tan pakay khushaala we.

Literal: Home is where a person is happy.

Happiness comes from inside. If a person's heart is content, then he is at home no matter where he lives or travels.

English equivalent: "Home is where the heart is."

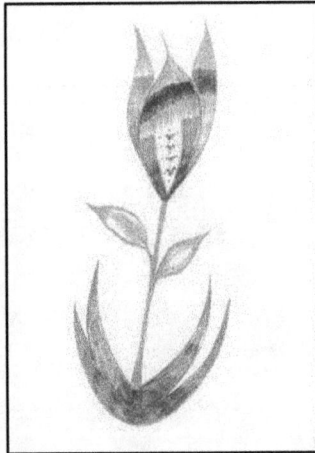

كه سل خويونه ئي نور شي
يو ئي د مور شي

Ka sal khoyuna yi nor she yao yi da mor she.

Literal: Even with a hundred traits, one will be of the mother.

Every person is unique, but a child naturally inherits at least a few qualities and traits from his parents and ancestors. This generational bond is always there.

English equivalents:
"Like father, like son" or "A chip off the old block."

د غله مخ تور وي.

Da-ghla mahk toor-wee.

Literal: *The face of a thief is always black.*

A bad person will eventually reveal his true nature, and people will eventually see it.

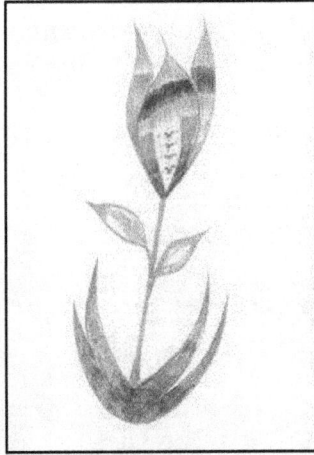

هغه سړی چې له هند نه دولت
او له افغانستان نه خپل سر راوړي،
په رښتیا ډېر هوښیار وي.

Hagha saray che la hind na dawlat
au la Afghanistan na khpal sar rawri,
pa rekhtiya der hokhiar day.

Literal: *A man is very clever if he brings back*
wealth from India, and his head from Afghanistan.

Said about someone who seems able to navigate
even the trickiest situations or problems.

(Note: Armies throughout history tried to conquer India
because of its wealth. When they passed through Afghanistan
on the way, they had to defend against Afghan warriors.)

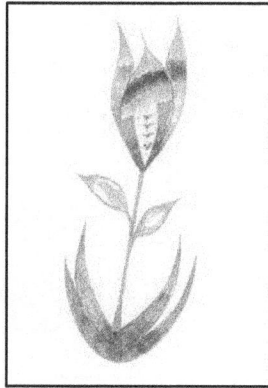

لعل په ايرو کښې نه پټيږي.

Laal pah eero ki na pataigey.

Literal: A jewel cannot remain hidden in ashes.

A person or thing with special skills, talents or qualities
is like a bright jewel, and cannot remain hidden for long.
One day these virtues will be seen by everyone.

اوږے د ډوډۍ تپار اوري.

Woogay da dodai tapaar awree

Literal: *A hungry person hears the clapping of the bread-making.*

Describes someone who has only one thing on his mind, and satisfying that need becomes an obsession. Such a person is attracted only to those things that seem to fulfill the need, whether real or imagined.

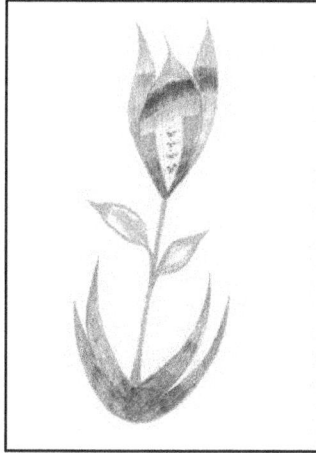

وطن په خلکو ښايسته وي.

Watan pah khalkoo shayestah we.

Literal: *One's nation is only made beautiful by the people in it.*

It is the people who make a place good or bad,
not the place itself. This is true from the
smallest villages to the largest countries.

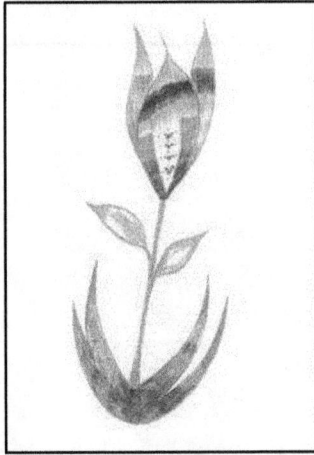

وریا شراب قاضي هم څښلي دي.

Warya sharab qazi hum sahaly de.

Literal: *Even a judge will taste free wine.*

Everybody loves free things. If something costs nothing
and is attractive, a person might try it even if he shouldn't.

(Note: A *qazi* (judge) is expected to be a pious and observant
Muslim, and therefore should not drink alcohol.)

یو په سل، او سل په خاورو.

Yow pa saal, aow saal pa khawrow.

Literal: *One is equal to one hundred,*
and one hundred is equal to dirt.

One brave person is better than a hundred cowards.

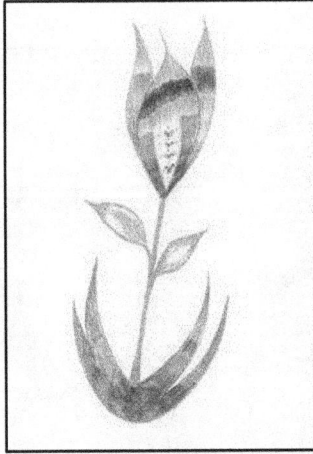

موږ د وږي له حاله څه خبردی.

Morh da wazhy la hala sa-khabar day.

Literal: *A fed person knows nothing about*
the situation of the hungry.

Some wealthy people don't think about the poor and needy,
because they have never felt hunger or wanted for anything.

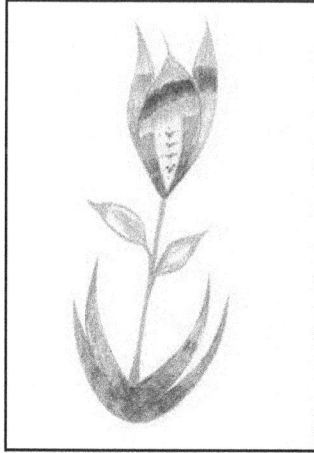

اوبه په کمزوري ځای ماتیږي.

Obah pah kamzore zai maategey.

Literal: Water spills over the dam at the weak point.

The weakest part of a person or thing usually is
the place where failure happens.

لمر په دوه ګتو نه پټیږی.

Lemar pa dwa gwato na pategy.

Literal: *The sun cannot be hidden by two fingers.*

Reality cannot be hidden by false explanations. The
truth cannot be hidden, just as it is impossible
to hold up two fingers and block the sun.

(English equivalent: "The truth will come out.")

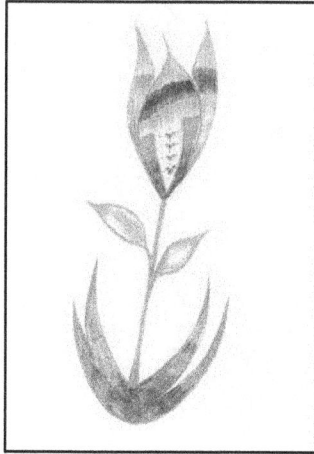

د هاتیانو سره ټانټي مه ژویه.

Da haatyaano sara taanti ma zoyaa.

Literal: *Don't chew straw with elephants.*

Try not to compete or fight directly against a powerful rival or enemy. It is better to find a more creative way to win.

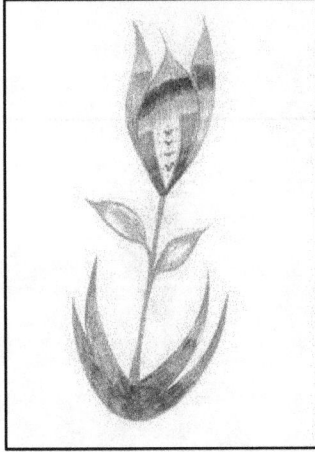

څه چي کرې هغه به ريبې.

Sa che karee hagha ba rebee.

Literal: *As you sow, so shall you reap.*

If you do good deeds you will be rewarded, just as if you sow
healthy seeds you will be rewarded with a bountiful harvest.
In the end people will get what they deserve as a result
of their actions, whether good or bad.

English equivalents: "What goes around, comes around"
and "The chickens will come home to roost."

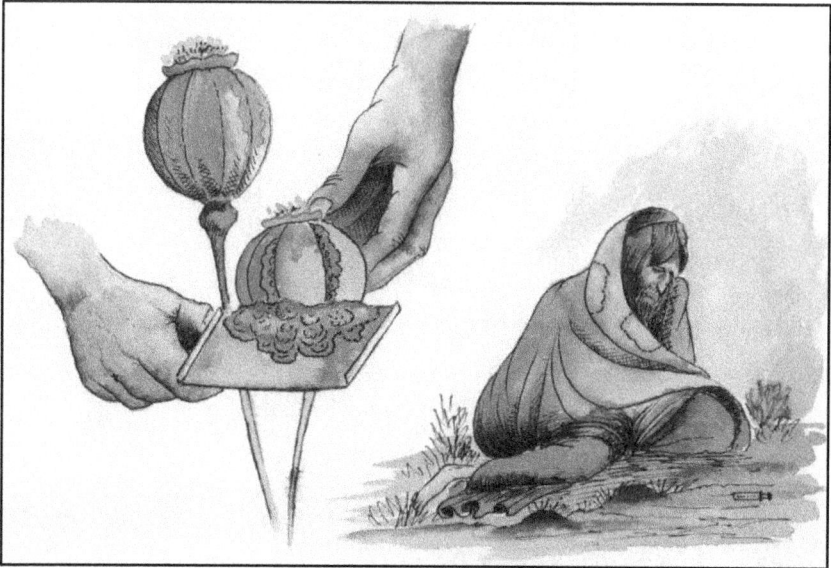

خداي د حقى لا ر ي مل د ىٕ.

Khodai tha hagay lahri mal day.

Literal: *God helps those who follow the true path.*

God is kind and merciful to those who are pious
and who do good things for others.

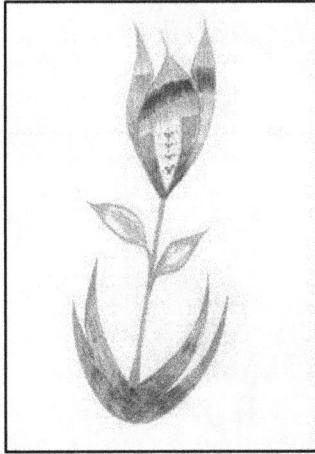

د توري پرهر رغېږي،
خو د ژبي نه رغېږي.

Da turey parhar raghegey,
kho da zhabay na raghegey.

Literal: *A sword wound heals,*
but the wound caused by a tongue cannot be healed.

People remember harsh statements and insults
much longer than they remember physical pain or injuries.

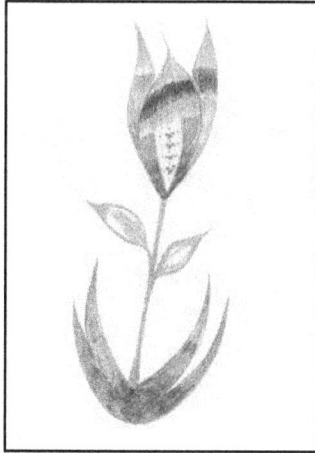

که کور پردی ده گیډه خو خپله ده.

Ka kor praday da gida kho khpala da.

Literal: *Even in someone else's home, your stomach is your own.*

It is bad manners to eat greedily when you are a guest.
Do not take advantage when someone does you a kind favor.

(*Note:* In Afghan culture, a host is duty-bound to serve a
guest. However, the guest is expected to show
restraint and good manners.)

لنډۍ حلال نه ببانک په سر.

Landay halaal na khaanak pa sar.

Literal: *The calf isn't even slaughtered yet
but the cookpot is on its head.*

Don't celebrate a win prematurely, because things can change.
At the very least, a celebration before the beginning or end
of an event looks awkward and ungracious.

English equivalents:
"Don't count your chickens before they hatch"
and "The opera isn't over until the fat lady sings."

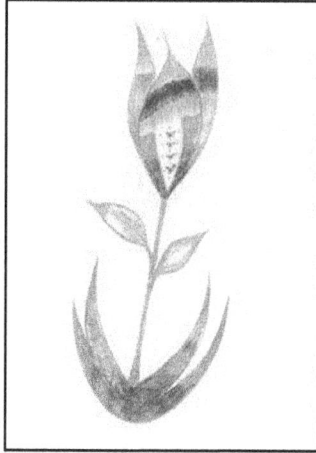

ورورې په کوؤ حساب تر مینځ.

Wroree ba kawoo hisaab tarmyanza.

Literal: *Keep a brotherly relationship by keeping accounts.*

It is important to deal honestly and equitably with
people and to document transactions properly.
This creates and maintains trust on all sides.

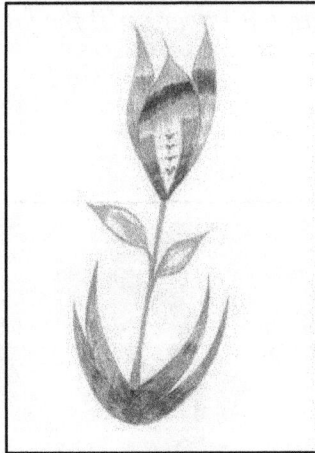

کوږ بار تر منزله نه رسیږي.

Kog baar tar manzala na rasigi.

Literal: *A tilted load won't reach its destination.*

Evil always loses and good prevails. If you have bad
intentions, ultimately you will be defeated. Only straight
and honest behavior leads to success in the end.

Also: If you try to play tricks on others, you will pay a price.

English equivalent: "Honesty is the best policy."

زوړنده ډوډۍ هیڅ چیرته نشته.

Zwaranda dodai hes charta nashta.

Literal: *Hanging bread is nowhere.*

Few things can be achieved without working for them,
and almost nothing comes without some cost or effort.
Hard work leads to success.

English equivalents: *"Money doesn't grow on trees"*
and "There is no free lunch."

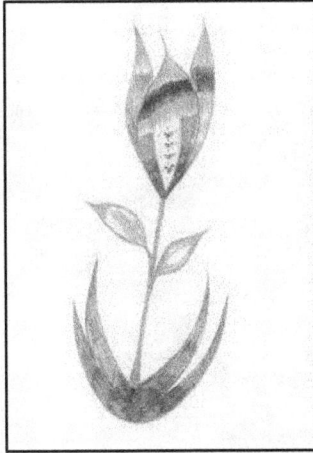

غوښه که وسوځي د پیتۍ نه ښه وي.

Ghwakha ka waswazee da pety na kha we.

Literal: Even meat that is burnt is better than grain.

It is better to have things of quality and value,
even if they are a bit old and worn.

(*Note:* Most Afghans love to eat meat and value it highly.
In the past, some Afghans looked down on people who
ate a lot of grain because it was considered inexpensive
and not savory enough for their liking.)

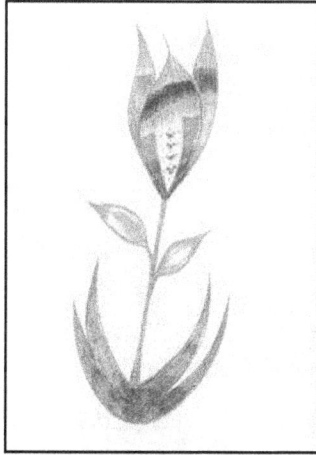

چي اختر تير شي نكريزى په دپوال وتپه.

Che akhtar ter she nakreezay pah diwaal watapa.

Literal: *After Eid, we might as well splat henna on the wall.*

Things are of no use if they are available, but not needed.
There is a usually a proper time to do things.

(*Note:* Many Afghans use henna in Eid holiday celebrations,
but use it much less often at other times of the year.)

شپ شپ مه کوه سم شفتالو وايه.

Shap shap ma kawa sam shaftaaloo waya.

Literal: Don't say "shap shap," say shaftaaloo (peach) properly.

Often used to lightly criticize a person who is being vague,
ambiguous, or is not expressing his purpose clearly.

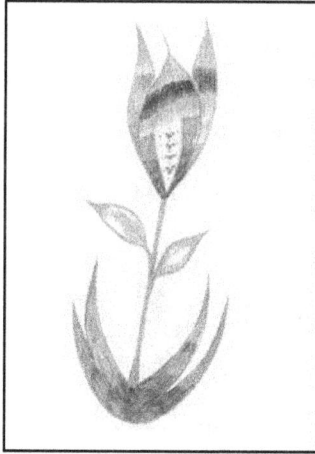

د هاتى په غوږ کښي ویده ئي.

Da haatee pa ghwag ki wedah yi.

Literal: *Sleeping in the elephant's ear.*

Describes an unwise person who is either not aware of what is going on around him, or does not understand it. A person who does not see reality risks danger or bad surprises.

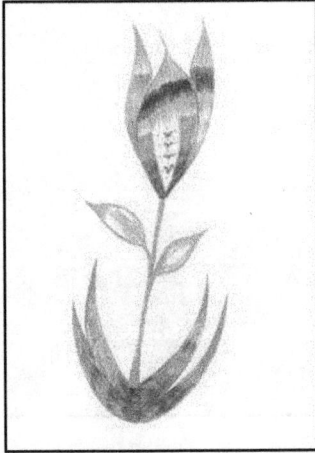

تور خر په صابون نه سپنیږي.

Tor khar pa sabun na spinaygee.

Literal: *A black donkey cannot be whitened by soap.*

No matter how hard you try, you cannot change someone's true nature. If a person is bad by nature, he cannot easily become good. You cannot bring a bad person to the right path simply by giving him advice.

که نه ځئ په شا به دې کْرم،
که نه خورې څه به دې کْرم.

Ka na zay pa shaa ba di kram
ka na khuray sa ba di kram.

Literal: *If you can't walk I can carry you on my back,*
but if you don't eat what can I do.

You can provide someone with an opportunity but you cannot
force them to accept it, no matter how logical it may be.

Also: There are some things you cannot help someone do.

English equivalent: *"You can lead a horse to water,*
but you can't make it drink."

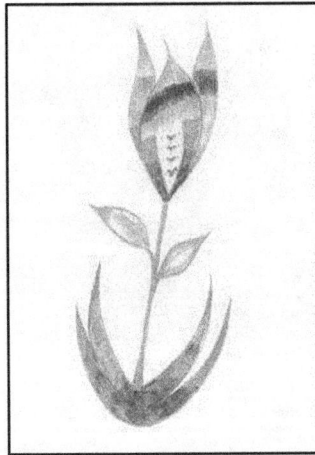

ملنگ ته يو ور پورې سل ورته خلاص.

Malang tah yo war pouray sal wartah khlas.

Literal: To a holy man, if one door closes a hundred will open.

Never get disappointed if one opportunity is missed. There
will always be others, even if you don't see them right away.
A wise person is hopeful, optimistic, and trusts in God.

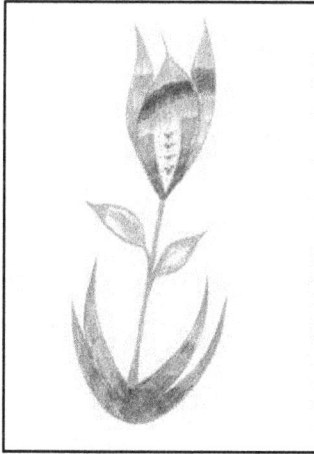

مار چیچلی د پري نه هم داریږی.

Maar chechalay da parey na hum daregee.

Literal: *Someone who has been bitten by a snake*
is even afraid of a rope.

A person who has had a very unpleasant or shocking
experience will not even come close to things
that remind them of that painful event.

د کم عقل دوست نه
هوښیار دښمن بنه دی.

Da kamaqal dost na okhyaar dushman kha day.

Literal: *A wise enemy is better than a foolish friend.*

A foolish friend is more dangerous to you than a
clever enemy, because you trust your friend and
he could lead you down the wrong path.

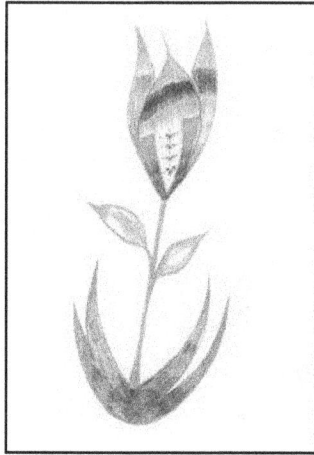

بيره د شيطان کار ده.

Berha da shaitaan kaar da.

Literal: *Haste is the work of the Devil.*

Don't rush things if it is not necessary.
A shortcut is not always the wise solution.

English equivalent: "Haste makes waste."

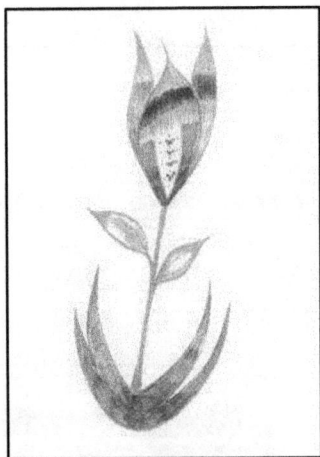

سل دي ومره يو دي مه مره.

Sal di omra yo di ma mra.

Literal: *A hundred can die, but let that one person not die.*

A good leader is always admired. People wish for his long life and hope that he never comes in harm's way.

Also: Legendary people are rarely born, and so we should protect and honor them.

پياز دې وي خو په نياز دې وي.

Pyaaz day wi kho pa nyaaz day wi.

Literal: *Be it but an onion, let it be given graciously.*

Happy gestures and good manners by a host are important in relations with family, friends, or guests. This is true no matter what is served, even if it is simple fare like bread and onions.

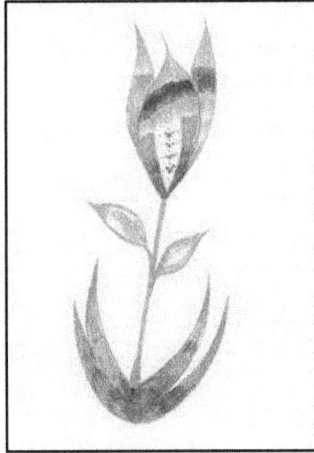

كاڼى چې په ځاى پروت وي دروند وي.

Kaany che pa zay prot we drund we.

Literal: A stone lying in its proper place is heavy.

Just as a stone resting in its own place cannot be easily moved,
a person who achieves a respected position is likely to stay
there if he keeps his dignity and acts within his bounds.

However, if that person interferes inappropriately in
outside affairs, it can damage his position or status.

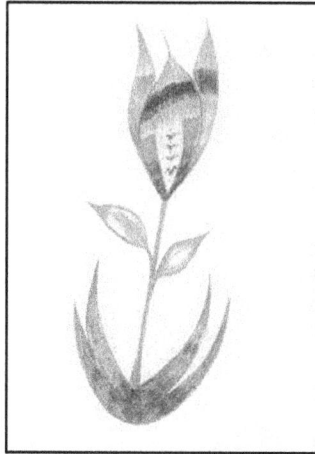

يو يي ګټي، سل يي څټي.

Yo yi gatee, sal yi saatee.

Literal: *One person earns, and feeds a hundred.*

Some Afghan families have a single person who earns
the livelihood for all members of the family,
and that person deserves great respect.

خواره خُله غوړی خبري.

Khwaara khula ghwary khabari.

Literal: *Poor mouth, rich words.*

This Matal describes people who make exaggerated boasts.
They cannot deliver on their promises, because they simply
are not capable of doing what they claim they can do.

English equivalents: "All hat and no cattle"
and "All talk and no action."

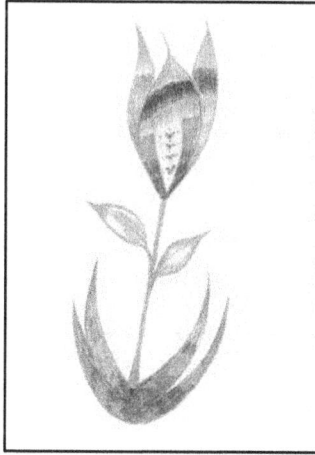

کږه خوله په سوک سميري.

Kaga khula pa sook samaigey.

Literal: *A crooked mouth is fixed by a punch.*

When a bad person refuses to budge or listen to reason, physical means may be used as a last resort. However, force is not the best solution to most problems. (See Matal #23)

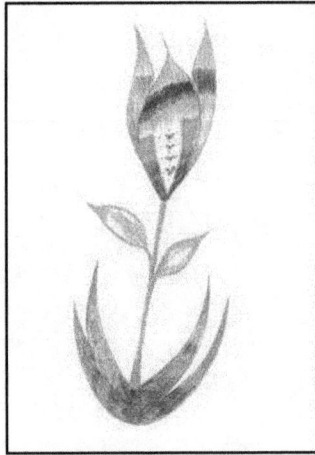

وائي يو څه او کوي بل څه.

Wayee yo sa ao kawee bal sa.

Literal: *Says one thing and does another.*

Describes hypocrites whose actions do not match their
words. Such people may pretend to have morals
or beliefs that they do not actually possess.

د زورور نه یا لری یا غلی.

Da zorawer na ya laray ya ghalay.

Literal: Stay silent or far from the powerful.

Avoid directly challenging someone who is more powerful
than you. Keep your distance and go about your own
business, rather than inviting trouble.

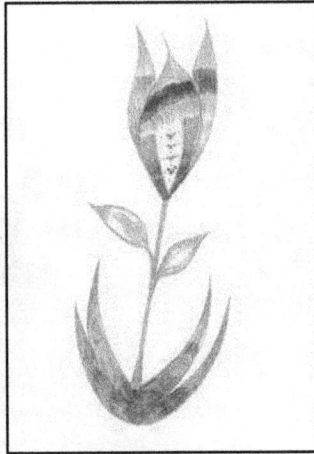

لـه پردي زوي نـه خپلـه لُور بنـه وي.

La pradey zooy na khpala lur kha we.

Literal: *Having your own daughter*
is better than having another's son.

The fruits of your own labor are always the sweetest.

(*Note*: Afghan culture traditionally values male offspring.
However, daughters are a special blessing too.)

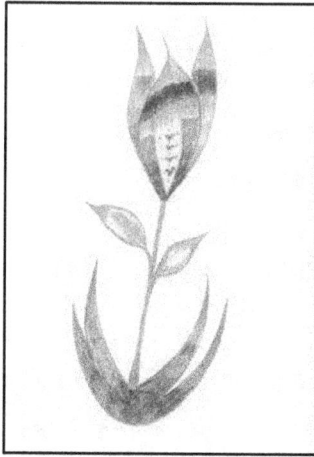

چي یارانه په شپتالو شوه نو ونشوه.

Che yaaraana pah shaptaaloo shwa no wanashwa.

Literal: *A friendship based on a peach is impossible.*

Sincere relationships and friendships should be unconditional.
If a person seeks friendship for a hidden motive, or tries to
buy someone's loyalty, it is not true friendship.

د کلي ووځه، خو له نرخه مه وځه.

Da keli wowuza, kho le nerkha me wuza.

Literal: *You can leave the village, but not your traditions.*

Respect and loyalty to your culture and heritage is important.
A person should remember and honor his roots and family
traditions, no matter where he is in the world or how
much wealth, fame or status he achieves.

English equivalent: "No matter where you go, there you are."

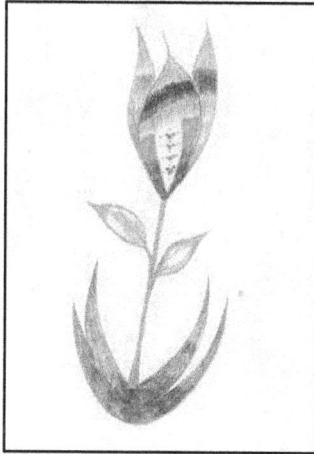

تورو تیارو پسی رڼا راځی.

Toro tyaro pase rana razi.

Literal: *After every darkness, there is light.*

Challenges, problems and bad times always will pass, and things will become better. Have faith and never lose hope.

English equivalent: "There is a light at the end of the tunnel."

داسي متل نشته چي ريښتيا نه وي.

Dasi matal nashta chi rekhtia na we.

Literal: *There is no Proverb which is not true.*

There is something that can be learned from every Proverb.
Proverbs (*Mataluna*) represent the collective cultural wisdom
of many people from generations past and present.

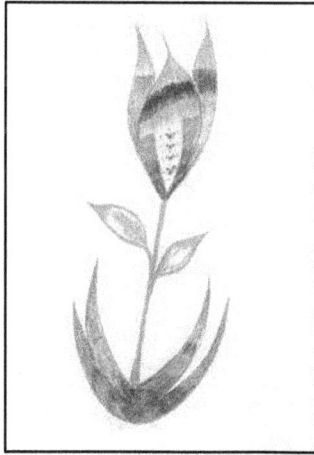

About the Author

د لیکوال په هکله

Captain Edward Zellem has served as a United States Navy officer for 27 years. He has won several national awards for his bilingual books of Afghan Proverbs, which are a personal project to support Afghan literacy. Captain Zellem began studying Dari in early 2010, and soon became captivated by the profound meanings and colorfulness of Afghan Proverbs. He started collecting them as a hobby and to help with his language studies. After deploying to Afghanistan later that year, he worked every day for a year and a half with many Afghan friends and colleagues in Kabul and Kandahar. Meanwhile, he continued to collect Afghan Proverbs as he heard and used them in his daily life in Afghanistan. After students at Marefat High School in Kabul offered to create illustrations, he decided to publish his collections and share them with the world. They eventually became the award-winning books *Zarbul Masalha: 151 Afghan Dari Proverbs*, the *Afghan Proverbs Illustrated* series, and now *Mataluna: 151 Afghan Pashto Proverbs*.

The author reviewing student art proposals at Marefat High School

About Marefat High School

د معرفت عالی لیسی په هکله

Marefat High School (MHS) was founded in 1994 in Pakistan to educate Afghan refugees. By 2001, more than 6000 Afghan male and female students were enrolled in different branches of the school in the cities of Rawalpindi, Attock, and Peshawar. At the beginning of the new political era in Afghanistan in 2001, MHS moved to Kabul and began educational programs in the 13th District, also known as Dashti Barchi – one of the poorest areas of the city.

Marefat High School, Kabul

Today, (2014) MHS has more than 3000 students enrolled. Since 2006, 100% of its graduates have successfully entered Afghan universities and other higher education institutions. More than 120 students have received scholarships for higher education in different countries around the world. For three successive years

Marefat High School has been ranked #1 in Afghanistan's nationwide university entrance exams. In the realm of education this achievement has made Afghan history in the modern era. MHS is one of the brightest beacons of hope in the entire Afghan educational system, even surpassing schools in wealthier areas that are far better funded and equipped.

Directed by a Board of Trustees, MHS is regarded as a model non-profit community initiative that provides quality education for Afghan children. Infrastructure, equipment, and the budget of the school are funded by a small tuition fee from each student. This is supplemented by contributions from Board members and other charitable donors from the community.

As of 2014, tuition at Marefat High School is approximately $230 U.S. dollars for an entire year, including books. Many Afghan families struggle to pay even this amount. Annually, private donors sponsor the educational expenses of more than 400 students in need through the "Marefat Charity Box."

MHS has nurtured many bright young talents in the fine arts, including painting, music, theater, story-writing, and poetry. One of the most successful projects by MHS students has been their illustration of Captain Zellem's *Zarbul Masalha* and *Mataluna* collections, with 50 works of original art in each book. The illustrations were created by young student artists between the ages of 14 and 16 in grades 7 to 10, guided by Marefat art masters and other faculty.

Progressive, integrated, community-based schools such as Marefat High School are the key to a brighter future for Afghanistan. Private and international donations to the school are always deeply appreciated.

More information about Marefat High School, including student essays and artwork, is available on its website in both Dari and English at http://www.marefatschool.org. The school's e-mail address is marefat12@gmail.com.

About The Editor

د ایډیټور په هکله

Hares Ahmadzai was born in Kabul, Afghanistan. He is a 2011 graduate of Kabul University Law School, and has served as a senior legal advisor and attorney for the NATO Rule of Law Mission in Afghanistan. He also has served as a senior cross-cultural advisor for U.S. forces in Afghanistan, and as a Pashto and Dari translator for several international organizations. Mr. Ahmadzai currently lives in the United States, where he continues his education.

حارث احمدزی په ۱۹۹۰ کال کی د کابل په ښار کی زیږیدلی ده او همدغه ښار کی یی زده کړی دی او د کابل پوهنتون د حقوقو او سیاسی علومو پوهنځی نه په کال ۲۰۱۱ کی د لیسانس په کچه فارغه شوی ده. هغه د ناتو سازمان د قانون دواکمنی او پیاورتیا په ځانګه کی د ستر حقوقی سلاکار او مدافع وکیل په توګه او مخکی له هغه د کلتوری سلاکار په توګه او همدارنګه له ۲۰۰۸ کال نه تر ۲۰۱۳ کاه پوری د پښتو او دری ژبی ژبارونکی او معلم په توګه په بیلابیلو نړیوالو بنستونو کی دنده تر سره کړی ده. حارث احمدزی دا مهال د امریکا متحده ایالاتو په ویرجینیا ایالت کی میشت او په لورو زده کړو بوخت دی.

About Qazi Ahmad Jan
د قاضی احمد جان په هکله

K.B. Qazi Ahmad Jan M.B.E. (1883-1951)

Pashto Writer, Grammarian, and Language Teacher
'The *Munshi* of Peshawar'

     Qazi Ahmad Jan is one of the pioneers and founders of Modern Pashto literature. Throughout his life he also was a great user and collector of Pashto Proverbs and idioms. Some of the proverbs in *Mataluna* were directly translated from the Pashto as found in his unpublished handwritten notebooks, and were generously donated to my book project by his grandson, **Ali Jan**. It is a rare privilege and honor to be able to include some of the Qazi's personal collection in *Mataluna: 151 Afghan Pashto Proverbs*. I am grateful to Ali Jan and his respected family for the opportunity to help promote and honor Qazi Ahmad Jan's works and legacy.

AHMAD JAN'S EARLY LIFE

Qazi ('*Judge*' in Pashto and Dari) Ahmad Jan's family originally came from Ghazni in Afghanistan. He was the son of another renowned and highly respected Afghan Qazi, Abdur Rahman Khan Muhammadzai. Qazi Abdur Rahman Khan was a famous 19th century Afghan judge, scholar and linguist who migrated from Afghanistan to pre-partition British India in the late 1800s. He was fluent in Arabic, English, Persian and Pashto, and is known as the first person to translate the Holy Bible's Old Testament into Pashto. Abdur Rahman Khan also translated John Bunyan's *The Pilgrim's Progress* and other works of English literature into Pashto.

Ahmad Jan was born in 1883 in Bannu, British India, and was educated at the Mission School built in Bannu by Christian missionaries. Demonstrating an early talent for languages, he became an interpreter for the British Army at a young age. After passing his certification exams in education from the University of Lahore, he moved permanently to Peshawar – the social and political metropolis of the frontier. He passed the *Munshi* (language teacher) Certification Examination with honors, and word of his talent spread.

TEACHING CAREER

At the time, learning Pashto was mandatory for all British civil servants, military officers and administrators in the districts where Pashto was spoken. This was particularly the case on the Northwest Frontier border between Afghanistan and British India (now part of Pakistan), where British officers were required to pass a tough military examination in the Pashto language. The young Ahmad Jan quickly became known as the teacher of choice in his capacity as a regimental *Munshi*, or language teacher.

One British officer, **Brigadier Mark C. A. Henniker**, singled out Ahmad Jan in his book *Memoirs of a Junior Officer* (Blackwood & Sons, 1951):

"I consulted my friends about a teacher, and all with one accord recommended Ahmad Jan...he was charming in every way and his methods of teaching quite unique."

Ahmad Jan's teaching career spanned over half a century, and he taught Pashto to thousands of British officials who served in the Northwest Frontier. Many of Ahmad Jan's students later rose to high positions in the Royal Indian Army and elsewhere. Brigadier Henniker goes on in his 1951 memoir to say that some of Ahmad Jan's young British officer students included the future **Field Marshal Bernard Law Montgomery**, the World War II hero of El Alamein; **Field Marshal Sir Claude J.E. Auchinleck**, the future Commander-in-Chief India; and **Field Marshal Archibald Percival Wavell**, the future Viceroy of India. All were stationed in Peshawar early in their military careers, and none would ever forget their young Pashto language teacher. Many years later, during Field Marshal Wavell's last visit to Peshawar as Viceroy of India, he made a special point of visiting Qazi Ahmad Jan in person to pay his respects.

WORKS OF QAZI AHMAD JAN

Ahmad Jan devoted his energies to developing and advancing Pashto grammar and literature right up to the time of his death in 1951. He took up serious writing in Pashto at a time when very little modern Pashto prose literature existed; most Pashtun writings at the time were often archaic and full of flowery Arabic and Persian expressions. Qazi Ahmad Jan introduced a new, simpler style of writing in his works that was idiomatic and modern, while at the same time retaining the natural flow and beauty of the Pashto language. He had complete command of Pashto Proverbs, and used them generously in his works.

Popularly known as 'Munshi Ahmad Jan' and 'The Munshi of Peshawar,' Ahmad Jan is perhaps most famous for popularizing the modern short story genre in the Pashto language. His short story compilation books *Hagha Dagha* (1929) and *Da Kissa Khane Gap* (1930) were published in both Pashto and English, and are still included in the curriculum for a master's degree in Pashto at the Pashto Academy in Peshawar. He was a strong advocate of education for women and girls, and set a personal example by sending his own two daughters to school to become doctors.

Other works by Qazi Ahmad Jan include the *Afridi Pashto Manual* (1909); *Pashto Made Easy* (1912); *How to Speak Pushtu* (1917); *Tarikh-e-Afghanistan* (1930), his Pashto translation of G.B. Malleson's 1879 book *History of Afghanistan*, and *Da kissa khane gap* (The Gossip of Qissa Khwani, 1930). Ahmad Jan also authored a variety of textbooks for studying advanced Pashto and interpreter examinations, and published a number of books in Pashto that he translated from Urdu and English, including Sir Thomas More's *Utopia*. Beginning in 1931, Ahmad Jan served as co-editor of the Pashto language journal *Staray Mashay*.

Ahmad Jan died peacefully at his home in Peshawar on October 19, 1951. He was beloved and deeply admired by the people of Peshawar, and thousands attended his funeral. Many of his Pashto dramas and plays had been broadcast every day on Peshawar radio stations for years.

AHMAD JAN'S MANUSCRIPTS AND NOTEBOOKS

A collection of rare books and manuscripts dating from the late 19th and early 20th centuries was recently discovered in Qazi Ahmad Jan's ancestral home, along with some manuscripts of his personal unpublished works. These manuscripts included collections of several hundred Afghan Pashto *mataluna* and idioms that Ahmad Jan had recorded and compiled in his own hand.

With the permission of his grandson Ali Jan and translation assistance by Ph.D candidate Noor ul Basar ('Aman'), a number of *mataluna* from Ahmad Jan's unpublished notebooks are translated and included in this book. It is my hope that this will help, even if in a small way, to help carry the legacy of the '*Munshi* of Peshawar' forward in the 21st century and beyond. I am proud to share some of Ahmad Jan's personal collection with the world in *Mataluna: 151 Afghan Pashto Proverbs*.

Qazi Ahmad Jan was many things, but by all accounts was always a Pashtun first and very proud of his Afghan heritage. His gravestone reads 'Afghan Muhammadzai' after his name.

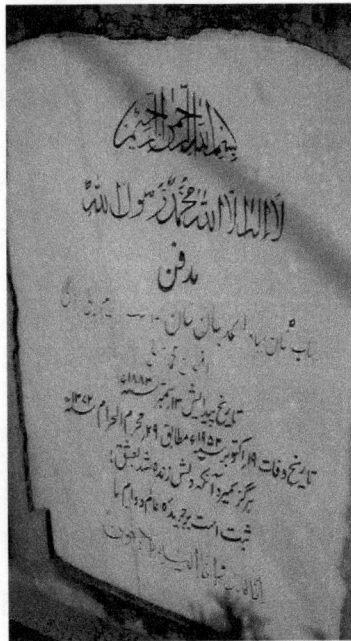

Gravestone of Qazi Ahmad Jan in Peshawar

لعل په ايرو کښې نه پټيږي.
Laal pah eero ki na pataigey.
A jewel cannot remain hidden in ashes.

About the Associação Internacional de Paremiologia/ International Association of Paremiology (AIP-IAP)

د AIP-IAP په هکله

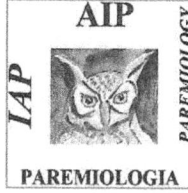

The AIP-IAP is a non-profit cultural institution based in the city of Tavira, located in the Algarve region of southern Portugal. The Association is dedicated to *Paremiology*, the scientific study of proverbs. As the only association of its kind in the world, the missions and purposes of the AIP-IAP include:

- To encourage international cooperation in Paremiology and related scientific areas;
- To establish action programs with educational officials, public and private;
- To encourage young researchers who are helping to defend, preserve and promote intangible cultural heritage;
- To organize national and international conferences in Paremiology;
- To promote studies in Paremiology, the scientific study of proverbs.

The quality and quantity of AIP-IAP activities and the published works of its members are recognized by world-renowned experts in global proverbs such as Paremiologists, Phraseologists, and Folklorists. This dynamism has resulted in support from the Municipality of Tavira; the Foundation for Science and Technology; the National Cultural Centre in Lisbon; the Secretary of State for Culture-Regional Directorate of Culture of the Algarve; and UNESCO, which has honored the AIP-IAP by granting it an Honorary Patronage. More information at http://www.aip-iap.org.

Also by Edward Zellem

Winner of three national book awards

Zarbul Masalha: 151 Afghan Dari Proverbs

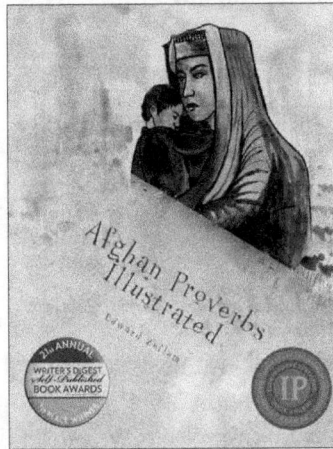

Afghan Proverbs Illustrated

*Now available in 14 languages through Amazon.com
and other major international booksellers*

Praise for _Zarbul Masalha_ and _Afghan Proverbs Illustrated_

"Ed's Afghan Proverb books are a personal project, and some people say that they _help win hearts and minds_. I have always thought that 'winning hearts and minds' is an inaccurate way to say it, because _winning_ implies that somebody also _loses_. Nobody loses here. I think Ed's Afghan Proverbs books _connect_ hearts and minds, which is a truly critical task."
   - General David H. Petraeus (U.S. Army, ret.)
   Former commander of U.S. and ISAF forces in Afghanistan

"These proverbs are a reminder of old traditions and folklore that have been passed from generation to generation. And they are a true delight for anyone who has been away or alienated from Afghanistan."
   - Leena Alam
   Award-winning Afghan actress and UNAMA Peace Ambassador

"Captain Zellem's collection is an outstanding work that underscores our common humanity."
   - Dwight Jon Zimmerman
   New York Times #1 best-selling author

"A delightful book...I commend Captain Zellem for honoring and selecting these glorious proverbs. I heartily recommend this book."
   - Bruce Cook
   5-Star review from ReadersFavorite.com

"All types of social and cultural learning and understanding are enriched through Proverbs."
   - Nancy Dupree
   Founder of the Afghanistan Centre at Kabul University (ACKU)

"Captain Edward Zellem has written one of the most remarkable books in recent memory about Afghanistan."
   - Veterans Radio Network

Translations of Edward Zellem's
Afghan Proverbs Illustrated

Now in over 70 countries

Greek

German

French

Russian

Polish

Portuguese

More Translations of Edward Zellem's
Afghan Proverbs Illustrated

Available through Amazon and other leading booksellers

Dutch

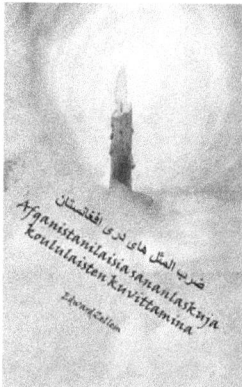

Finnish

Italian

Swedish

Spanish

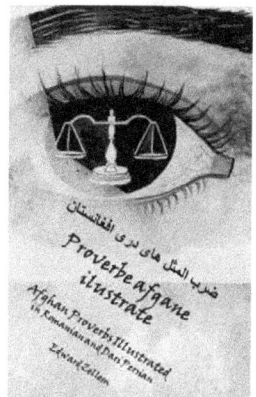

Romanian